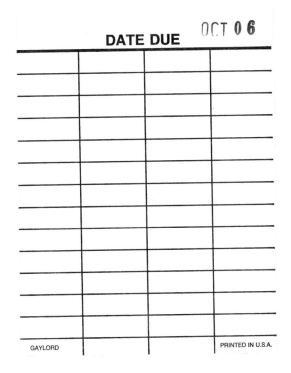

DATE DUE OCT 0 6

GAYLORD | | | PRINTED IN U.S.A.

The Music
Library

The Instruments
of Music

Other books in this series include:

The Music
Library

The Instruments
of Music

by Stuart A. Kallen

LUCENT
BOOKS®

THOMSON
™
GALE

San Diego • Detroit
• London • Munich

THOMSON
———✳———™
GALE

LIBRARY OF CONGRESS CATALOGING-IN-PUBLICATION DATA

Kallen, Stuart A., 1955–
    The instruments of music / by Stuart A. Kallen.
        p. cm. — (The music library)
Includes bibliographical references (p.).
    ISBN 1-59018-127-1 (hardback : alk. paper)
    1. Musical instruments—Juvenile literature. [1. musical instruments.] I. Title. II. Music
library (San Diego, Calif.)
    ML460 .K25 2003
    784.19—dc21

2001006609

Printed in the United States of America

• Contents •

• Foreword •

In the nineteenth century English novelist Charles Kingsley wrote, "Music speaks straight to our hearts and spirits, to the very core and root of our souls. . . . Music soothes us, stirs us up . . . melts us to tears." As Kingsley stated, music is much more than just a pleasant arrangement of sounds. It is the resonance of emotion, a joyful noise, a human endeavor that can soothe the spirit or excite the soul. Musicians can also imitate the expressive palate of the earth, from the violent fury of a hurricane to the gentle flow of a babbling brook.

The word music is derived from the fabled Greek muses, the children of Apollo who ruled the realms of inspiration and imagination. Composers have long called upon the muses for help and insight. Music is not merely the result of emotions and pleasurable sensations, however.

Music is a discipline subject to formal study and analysis. It involves the juxtaposition of creative elements such as rhythm, melody, and harmony with intellectual aspects of composition, theory, and instrumentation. Like painters

mixing red, blue, and yellow into thousands of colors, musicians blend these various elements to create classical symphonies, jazz improvisations, country ballads, and rock-and-roll tunes.

Throughout centuries of musical history, individual musical elements have been blended and modified in infinite ways. The resulting sounds may convey a whole range of moods, emotions, reactions, and messages. Music, then, is both an expression and reflection of human experience and emotion.

The foundations of modern musical styles were laid down by the first ancient musicians who used wood, rocks, animal skins—and their own bodies—to re-create the sounds of the natural world in which they lived. With their hands, their feet, and their very breath they ignited the passions of listeners and moved them to their feet. The dancing, in turn, had a mesmerizing and hypnotic effect that allowed people to transcend their worldly concerns. Through music they could achieve a level of shared experience that could not be found in other forms of communication. For this reason, music has always been part of religious endeavors, from ancient Egyptian religious ceremonies to modern Christian masses. And it has inspired dance movements from kings and queens spinning the minuet to punk rockers slamming together in a mosh pit.

By examining musical genres ranging from Western classical music to rock and roll, readers will find a new understanding of old music and develop an appreciation for new sounds. Books in Lucent's Music Library focus on the music, the musicians, the instruments, and on music's place in cultural history. The songs and artists examined may be easily found in the CD and sheet music collections of local libraries so that readers may study and enjoy the music covered in the books. Informative sidebars, annotated bibliographies, and complete indexes highlight the text in each volume and provide young readers with many opportunities for further discussion and research.

Introduction

The Sounds of Music

In the most basic terms, music is sound transmitted by vibrations traveling through the air. But music can be many things to many people. It can be a songbird chirping in a tree, a cicada rhythmically rubbing its hind legs together, a person singing in the shower, or a wildly popular rock group performing before tens of thousands of people. Above all, music communicates emotion, whether it comes from the serenely peaceful sound of a single wooden flute or the manic, angry hammering of a heavy metal band. And whether the music is coming from a lone performer or one-hundred-piece symphony orchestra, instruments act as extensions of the feelings, inspirations, and spirits of the musicians playing them.

It is said that, like snowflakes, no two musical performances are alike. The same may be said of musical instruments. Composed of wood, metal, animal skin, plastic, or parts of plants, each instrument vibrates at a slightly different pitch and timbre, and with subtle variations of tone. Even two seemingly identical guitars of the same model and the same manufacturer will add slightly different colorations to the sound of music. This is why some people are as interested in collecting musical instruments as they are in playing them.

Often made from materials that were once alive, such as spruce, goat skin, or bamboo, musical instruments may be thought of as extensions of nature. And the sounds played upon them may remind listeners of leaves rustling in the breeze, an animal bleating in the forest, or rumbling waves of thunder on the horizon. Those made from brass, plastic, or computer chips resonate with their own range of sound and texture, invoking the high spirits of a marching band, the sounds of the city after midnight, or even the noises of a spaceship landing in a field.

While it is hard to separate instruments from musicians, percussion, winds, brass, keys, and strings are tools that have influenced the music people have composed over the centuries. Thousands of years ago when ancient societies had access only to drums and the human voice, the music embodied the sounds of the tribal beat. In the age of Mozart and Beethoven, popular music reflected the exhalations of the violin, cello, oboe, clarinet, and trumpet of the symphony orchestra.

Today, guitars, drums, and computerized keyboards are used to express the wide range of emotions found in modern society. While the idea of the angry young rock singer may be cliché, without the electric guitar blaring through a wall of screaming amplifiers, that fury would be much harder to demonstrate to a large audience.

Whether it comes from a single instrument or the combined sounds of an orchestra, music has the power to emotionally move listeners.

Above all, instruments are extensions of what composers, songwriters, and musicians hear inside their heads—and feel in their souls. As Beethoven wrote on the top of the sheet music when he finished his renowned Ninth Symphony, "From the heart it came, from the heart may it go."[1] And utilizing the emotionally charged sounds of the piano, violin, cello, clarinet, oboe, flute, trumpet, and dozens of other instruments, the orchestra can deliver Beethoven's musical vision straight to the hearts of the audience.

Chapter One

Percussion

Music, unlike any other art form, takes place in time. A painting may hang on a wall for a thousand years, but live music passes in a matter of minutes. Since music and time are intertwined, it is the rhythm that keeps a song moving on its proper course. Musical rhythm may be held by the clapping of hands, the bounce of a bow across violin strings, the thumping of a bass guitar, or even the crash of waves on a beach. It is the rhythmic vibrations of drums and percussion instruments, however, that most often hold music's place in time.

At its most basic level, a percussion instrument is anything that produces a sound when hit with a hand or other implement such as a stick or mallet. The simplest percussive instruments are sticks, rocks, or other natural objects pounded together. Percussive instruments may also be hit with various devices. Bells are rung by the center clapper swinging back and forth. Xylophones are hit with rubber mallets. Rattles rely on shaken beads, gravel, or ball bearings. Bass drums are pounded with drumsticks. And the Tibetan *damaru* is shaken rapidly, causing a knotted chord to thrum on both sides of a drumhead.

Idiophones

Whatever their form, percussive devices are the oldest instruments known to the human race and date back twenty millennia or more. Percussion instruments that do not have to be tuned, such as gongs, castanets, triangles, and woodblocks, are called idiophones. These instruments resonate and are played by striking, scratching, scraping, rubbing, and shaking.

The first idiophones were made from rocks, sticks, animal skulls, antlers, bones, seashells, and plants such as dried gourds whose seeds rattled when shaken. Their rhythmic patterns, especially when established by more than one player, had the ability to change the mood of the listeners and cause them to get up and dance. As such, idiophones were originally played by shamans and religious practitioners, and their music had a deep religious significance. As former Grateful Dead drummer Mickey Hart writes in *Drumming at the Edge of Magic*:

We have idiophones dating back to 20,000 B.C. that are daubed with red ochre [paint], a decora-

Rhythm and Noise

Mickey Hart was the drummer for the Grateful Dead for more than thirty years. As one of the most renowned rock drummers in the world, he spends his time documenting ancient rhythmic traditions throughout the world. In Drumming at the Edge of Magic, *Hart explores the roots of drumming.*

In the beginning was noise. And noise begat rhythm. And rhythm begat everything else. . . .

Strike a membrane with a stick, the ear fills with noise—unmelodious, inharmonic sound. Strike it a second time, a third, you've got rhythm.

Fifty thousand years ago noise and rhythm came together and we began to talk. . . . We were toolmakers extraordinaire, with a significant repertoire of grunts, squeaks, barks, hums, rasps, growls—poised on the edge of a cultural explosion that would pitch us out of nature.

Everywhere we looked we saw rhythms, patterns moving through time—in the cycles of the stars and the migrations of animals, in the fruiting and withering of the plants we gathered and eventually domesticated. Rhythm was the heart of mystery. . . .

Imagine the soundscape fifty thousand years ago. Noise meant danger, possibly death, an understanding rooted in the oldest parts of the brain, in the fight-or-flight programs that activate the [adrenaline glands], preparing the organism for immediate action.

This is what the Hindus knew on a cosmic scale: there is terror in noise.

And in that terror there is also power. In one of her books, Jane Goodall tells of a chimpanzee who discovers the powerful effect of two empty kerosene cans banged together. Within weeks he becomes the troupe's dominant male.

Rhythm and noise. That's where drummers come from.

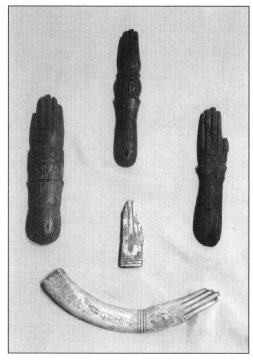

These rattles from ancient Egypt are examples of early idiophones.

are believed to have been pounded to generate good luck before a hunt. Gourd rattles might have blessed a baby's birth. The slow rhythm of a stick clacking across a ridged stone surface may have helped send a fallen warrior into the afterlife.

In the ancient tradition, idiophones can be anything that can be played rhythmically, including the human body. In the Amazon rain forest, indigenous tribes still perform a ritual fire dance while slapping their legs with their hands. Natives of the Andaman Islands near India accompany traditional dances with a sounding board—a board lying on the ground supported on one side by a rock and stamped with the heel of the foot. And nearly every culture on Earth has some sort of idiophonic device, whether simple or complicated, as Hart writes:

> In Papua New Guinea you'd hear the "clap clap" of shells and crayfish claws, while in Zaire the Vili [tribe] would slap the thick expanse of their thighs with hollowed out [gourds]. . . . *Bwop . . . Bwop.*

> The San [people] of South Africa fill springbok [small deer] ears with pebbles and wear them on their ankles. In West Africa the top of a gourd is removed and the player pounds the open end against the ground, producing a nice percussive *pop!* as the trapped air vibrates against the fruit's tough skin.

tion most scholars believe indicates a sacred usage. But the first "document" of percussion's connection with the sacred doesn't show up until . . . around 15,000 B.C., when an anonymous artist, working in a limestone cavern in southwestern France, painted our first known picture of a musician. Known as the dancing sorcerer (or shaman) of Les Trois Frères . . . this picture has been interpreted by scholars as representing a man wearing the skin of an animal and playing some kind of instrument, possibly . . . a concussion stick.[2]

Idiophones such as woolly mammoth skulls and bighorn sheep antlers

The gourd can be kept intact and beaten with sticks or chopped in half, placed hollow down in the water, and struck. In northern Haiti players put metal thimbles on their fingers to excite the gourd's body, while in the Solomon Islands topless gourds are plunged in and out of water, making a sound that one writer transliterates as "uh/ah/uh/ah/uh/ah."[3]

The Bells

While percussionists have used natural objects to play traditional music for thousands of years, musical bells did not come into fashion until around 2000 B.C. Bells are cup-shaped idiophones made from wood or metal that contain a clapper that strikes the body of the device to produce a ringing sound. The clapper might also be handheld, an object such as a drumstick.

Some types of modern African music, such as *soukous,* rely on the driving ring of funnel-shaped double bells to keep rhythm in large bands that might feature several drummers, horn players, guitarists, and singers. The constant ring of the bell acts as a time-keeping metronome—like a conductor in a symphony orchestra—to keep the musicians on the beat.

The agogo, *a type of double bell, originated in Africa and has been adapted by cultures around the world.*

Another type of African double bell, the *agogo,* has traveled around the world and been adapted by cultures on several continents, as Töm Klöwer writes in *The Joy of Drumming:*

> Black iron bells are predominantly played in African music, in places such as Togo, the Cameroons, Nigeria, and the Congo. . . . They were taken to the Caribbean and Brazil by the Bantus (who call the instrument "ngonge," which means "time and respect"), and the Yorubas (who call it "agogo"), as part of their African culture. The agogo is used in the Brazilian [religious] rituals, as well as in Brazilian street samba. This bell is characterized by a clear, bright sound, rich in harmonics. . . . It comes in many different versions. The clicking sounds you often hear in Brazilian music are made by briefly pressing the bells together with the left hand. The handle acts as a spring so that the bells return to their original position.[4]

The wooden *agogo,* used in samba music, is similar to the metal version, but has a softer, more soothing tone. The cowbell, a more common type of bell, can be seen attached to rock-and-roll drum kits throughout the world. In recent decades, rock drummers have also added various bells commonly used in Latin American salsa music.

Smaller bells are also incorporated into idiophonic instruments. The traditional "jingle bells" may be found on sticks or leather straps. Smaller bells have a higher pitch, while large bells emit lower tones. Similar in sound, wrist and ankle bracelets originated in India and today are used by dancers on stage or even at rock concerts.

Rattles

Rattles, like bells, were common in ancient cultures throughout the world. The first rattles were made from plants, small woven baskets, animal teeth, seashells, and plant seeds—a custom that continues today. The part they play in traditional North American music is discussed by Bernard S. Mason in *Drums, Tomtoms, and Rattles:*

> Rattles are almost . . . indispensable to dancing in the eyes of most Indian tribes. . . . They are as universal among the Indians as . . . drums and usually hold a place of prestige almost equal to that of the drum. Not all dances call for rattles but some rituals cannot be performed without them; in fact, some use no drums at all, the only sound being the clicking of the rattles in the hands of the dancers.[5]

The most common rattles are made from gourds, but rattles may also be assembled from buffalo horns, birch bark, turtle shells, seashells, coconuts, and even tin cans. These instruments are filled with gravel, seeds, teeth, and other rattling devices. The exteriors of the rattles may be painted with symbolic designs, decorated with intricate beadwork, or have feathers or animal hair attached.

Rattles have religious significance for many people across the globe. In a creation story from Guinea, the goddess Crehu gave a calabash gourd and white pebbles to a tribesman and told him to put the gravel into the gourd and call it a "maraca." That word has followed the rattling instrument around the world where maracas are used by traditional musicians, Latin American orchestras, and rock bands alike.

Other religious uses for the rattle are discussed by James Blades in *Percussion Instruments and Their History*:

The gourd rattle . . . remains an important instrument of the North American shaman. These priests, traditionally men of extraordinary talents, are well-trained in poetry, medicine, philosophy, languages, athletics, conjuring and the art of music. When supplicating their gods, they have often moved men to tears with the magic of their poetry and music, accompanied in most cases with rattles.

The rattle is an important item of the equipment used by the African [healer]. During the operation of ejecting an evil spirit, the "medicine" man and his assistant shake their rattles and growl throughout the whole performance, in order to terrify the spirit and render the patient more susceptible to the uncanny influence of the ceremony. On occasions of this nature the illu-

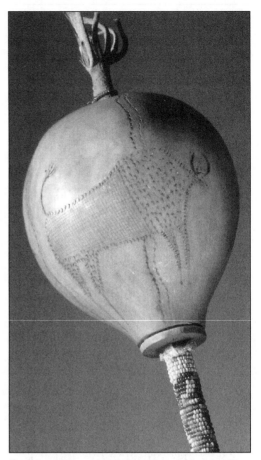

Rattles play an integral role in traditional Native American music.

sion is often intensified by the use of rattles adorned with fetishes or the carved head of a supernatural being, while the various complaints are treated with separate rhythms.[6]

Outside of Africa, rattles are used in Korean shrines by Buddhist priests who attract the gods by striking rattles with small sticks. In Brazil, indigenous people believe that the gods live within certain rattles. And in Lapland, some believe that the devil dwells in rattles.

Gongs

Like rattles, gongs have been used for centuries throughout the world for religious purposes. In their simplest form, gongs are metal discs with turned rims that resonate a single long, reverberating note when struck with a stick, mallet, or other device. The cymbals that rock drummers use are based on the ancient gong that probably originated in Southeast Asia around the ninth century. The term

The Rainmaker

Some idiophones are used to make sound effects that imitate waterfalls, crickets chirping, teeth chattering, and even the sound of water glug-glugging from a bottle. In The Joy of Drumming, *Töm Klöwer writes about one of the more popular idiophones, the rainstick or rainmaker.*

The precursor of the rainmaker, the guasa, comes from the African and Latin American cultures. The guasa is a shaking tube about three feet long, plaited from fibers, and filled with light seeds. When the tube is turned upside down, the seeds flow down, making a rustling sound. It is used in the music of the Curulao in [Colombia].

The modern rainmaker consists of a cylindrical tube, sometimes made of metal, with many pins attached, in a spiral formation, to the inside wall. The small beads inside flow down slowly and evenly when the tube is rotated. The impression of rain falling is imitated perfectly by this ingenious construction of plastic and metal. In [some models] . . . you can even hear a sound like the rushing of the wind: at each end of the tube there is a cap, which has a small hollow space. When you cover the two hollow spaces with your hand and then shake the balls down, you can imitate the sound of the wind by opening and closing the palms of your hands.

Another version of the rainmaker is made of transparent plastic, revealing the way in which the instrument works. Plastic beads gradually filter down to the bottom through plastic discs with holes. The snake rainmaker . . . also produces a very delicate sound. It is used predominantly as a shaking instrument. . . . [Another type of rainmaker] is an almost archaic, yet commonly found, type . . . made from a hollow cactus with sharp thorns on the loose inside, which produce a delicate, warm sound.

A man plays a gong during a religious ceremony at a Bali temple.

"gong" itself is from the Malay language.

Gongs have summoned Buddhists to meditation for centuries, and some museums display gongs that are nearly one thousand years old. In *Drums Through the Ages,* Charles L. White describes ancient beliefs concerning gongs:

> Drinking from a gong bound a man to his oath. Washing oneself in a gong assured good health. The gong could frighten away evil spirits, cure the sick, bring favorable winds. Certain gongs were held in such high esteem that they were given proper names. Fine gongs were high in value . . . and

they were considered a sign of wealth and rank. They have been used as currency.[7]

In the eighteenth century, gongs from China were imported to the West and were used by symphony orchestras. Gongs may be heard today in a wide variety of venues ranging from the dance music of India to the recordings of rock bands such as Pink Floyd, the Grateful Dead, and others. Like most other idiophones, gongs have passed from their ancient magical roots to travel around the world. While doing so, they have provided rhythm and sound to celebrations from the religious to rock and roll.

Speaking with Drums

While idiophones are the most ancient of instruments, drums probably did not appear in human history until around 4500 B.C. Like bells, rattles, and gongs, however, drums have been used for a wide variety of purposes from the mystical to the militaristic.

The earliest drums were most likely made from logs. Instruments called slit gongs, or slit drums, were used to send messages across the African jungle until recent times. Slit drums are hollowed-out logs from three feet to forty feet in length with long slits carved into the tops. Various perpendicular cuts along the slit give the drums different tones when they are beaten with mallets. As Blades writes: "The double note of the early log drums was probably one of man's first steps in instrumental melody."[8]

Like other ancient instruments, slit drums are imbued with magical beliefs, and the hollowed-out slits where the tones emerge are considered home to deities, the dead, or sons yet unborn. In addition, slit drums have long been used as a means to send messages over great distances, as Blades writes:

Apart from its magical significance, the large slit drum has been, and remains, important as a means of communication in [some] tribes. As a message drum it continues to "speak" to a great number of people in the way it has spoken to their forefathers for centuries past.

In remote parts of Central Africa, the signals transmitted by means of a drum language (Bush Telegraph) consist of a form of Morse code. Strokes of differing strength and pitch provide a form of "telephonic" conversation, by which news travels at considerable speed. The drum languages are as numerous as the almost innumerable languages and dialects of Africa itself. The early explorers were confounded by the obvious advanced knowledge of their movements over large areas.[9]

The Ancient Drum

Slit drums are the largest and loudest idiophones. In this way they resemble modern drums, which are classified as membranophones because they consist of animal skins, or membranes, stretched across the ends of hollow cylinders.

The earliest drums were tiny instruments made from the skins of fish, lizards, or snakes. Tanned hides from rabbits, sheep, goats, pigs, mules, cows, dogs, or even wolves came into fashion in later centuries.

This early African drum was made from wood and elephant skin.

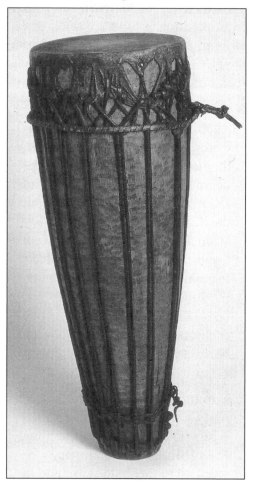

Drum cylinders might be hollow tree stumps, clay bowls, seashells, or even human skulls—any device that resonates and amplifies the sound when the skin is hit. To those who love to drum, covering a cylinder with a membrane was an important step in human history. As Hart writes: "For me the discovery of the percussive possibilities of skin ranks right up there with the discovery of fire and the invention of the wheel."[10]

Mesopotamian art shows that simple clay drums existed five thousand years ago. Ancient female figurines found in Mesopotamia around 2300 B.C. show women playing small, round frame drums similar to the tambourine. Layne Redmond describes such a drum in *When the Drummers Were Women:*

> The ancient frame drum . . . is primarily a wheel-shaped drum whose diameter is much wider than the depth of its shell. It is round and shaped like a grain sieve, and both the drum and the sieve probably share the same origin. Both [were symbolic in ancient times] of the feminine, fertility, grain, the moon, the sun, and the primordial first body of water. Ritual and symbolic connections between the two reach back into prehistory.

> The frame drum most often has a skin on only one side but sometimes it may have skins stretched across both sides. Bells or jingling and rattling implements may be attached to the inside rim, and in

ancient times were believed to add to the drum's power to purify, dispel, and summon. The drums were often painted red, the color of blood, or sometimes green, the color of vegetation. Throughout the ancient world, these were the primordial colors of life. Mystical designs and symbols might also be painted on the skin head or the wooden frame. Threads or ribbons knotted with ritual prayers or chants often hung from them.[11]

Over the centuries, membranophonic drums have been developed on nearly every continent, and at least fifty different types can be found in places such as Asia, Brazil, the Middle East, and North America. The African continent probably has more kinds of drums than any other. As Blades writes: "Every [tribe] inhabiting the vast territory has . . . had a drum of some description during its history. No indigenous musical instrument remains as widely spread or as greatly used."[12]

Those who could play drums with skill were elevated to leadership positions within tribes, as the instruments were thought to cure disease or inflict pain and bad luck. Ceremonies such as rain dances, hunting rituals, and war councils were conducted to the beat of the drum.

The Conga

With such a long history, drums have been made in every conceivable size and shape, from the towering fifteen-foot-tall African war drum to the tiny tambourine no bigger than a human hand. Common cylinder shapes include the cone and double cone, the hourglass, the goblet, the barrel, frame drums, and the bowl-shaped kettledrum. The membranes, or drumheads, are stretched taut and held in place by tacks, metal frames, rope, leather cords, screws, or other similar devices.

There are three basic drum styles—the single-head, closed at the bottom, such as the African kettledrum; the single-head open at one end, such as the bongo drum; and the double-head with skins on each end, typically found

Young boys play single-head conga drums on a Brazilian street corner.

on snares, toms, and other drums found on modern drum sets.

Some of the most common drums in use today have their roots in Africa. The conga, a single-head, barrel-shaped drum popular with Latin rock and jazz musicians, is descended from the African *makuta* drums of the Congo region. These drums may be found in concert halls, on stage with Latin pop sensation Ricky Martin, or on street corners where Cuban carnival groups perform rumba music. Conga players can coax various sounds from the drums such as bass tones, the open tone and open slap, the muffled tone and muffled slap, and various finger and palm tones.

Drums and the Military

Drums have long been used to signal soldiers when battle was about to begin. In 1287, Italian explorer Marco Polo witnessed a battle between the armies of Mongol warrior Kublai Khan and that of his rival Nayan. On the "Kublai Khan in Battle, 1287" website, Polo describes the battle, beginning with sound of the huge, five-foot-tall kettledrums known as Naccara.

[W]hen] all were in battle array on both sides . . . and nothing remained but to fall to blows, then might you have heard a sound arise of many instruments of various music, and of the voices of the whole of the two hosts loudly singing. For this is a custom of the [Mongols], that before they join battle they all unite in singing and playing . . . a thing right pleasant to hear.

And so they continue in their array of battle, singing and playing in this pleasing manner, until the great Naccara (*giant battle drums*) of the Prince is heard to sound. As soon as that begins to sound the fight also begins on both sides; and in no case before the Prince's Naccara sounds dare any commence fighting.

So then, as they were thus singing and playing, though ordered and ready for battle, the great Naccara of the Great Khan began to sound. And that of Nayan also began to sound. And thenceforward the din of battle began to be heard loudly from this side and from that. And they rushed to work so doughtily [marked by fearless recognition] with their bows and their maces [and] with their lances and swords . . . that it was a wondrous sight to see.

A three-drum set, known collectively as congas, adds a bass-toned *tumba,* which is similar in shape but larger than a conga, and the higher-pitched *quinto,* which is smaller. Quality congas are made from hardwoods, although some modern drums are made from fiberglass and plastic. The drumhead is tanned cow or donkey hide from one-sixteenth to one-eighth of an inch thick. The heads can be tuned—that is, their pitch may be changed—by tightening or loosening screws attached to both the drum body and the metal tension ring that holds the skin in place.

Kettledrums and Timpani

While conga drums have mostly remained in the realms of Latin and rock music, kettledrums have had the distinction of crossing the cultural barrier from Africa, India, and the Middle East to western Europe in the sixteenth century. Kettledrums started out as single-head instruments stretched over clay or copper bowls. White describes their military use in India many centuries ago:

> Some of the early kettle-shaped drums used by the tribes of India were made of pine wood hollowed out into hemispheric form and then equipped with heads of bull hide. Inside the wooden shell of these ancient Hindu drums were fitted bells of bronze. The drum was held high in the air and beaten in a loud and terrifying manner during battles, for the purpose of frightening the enemy. The bells were jingled by hitting [them]

against the side of the drum. This was thought to create magic and bring good luck and victory.[13]

By the fifteenth century, kettledrums accompanied all royal parades in India. Bands that played for the emperor used massive instruments whose heads were about five feet in diameter and stretched across huge silver bowls weighing nearly 450 pounds each. A single bull elephant was used to carry two of the drums and two drummers, each wielding his own pair of silver drumsticks used to pound out a loud, rumbling explosion of rhythm. Smaller drums were mounted on each side of camels' humps while one drummer sat in the middle and played both.

By this time, the kettledrum had been brought to Europe, probably by Arab traders. Like their Eastern counterparts, the Europeans recognized the value of the thundering drums in warfare. As such, their popularity quickly spread across the continent from Germany to Russia to Great Britain.

The kettledrum eventually shrank in size to resemble the modern tambour, or timpani. These drums were adapted for symphony orchestras in the eighteenth century by classical composers such as Johann Sebastian Bach and George Frederic Handel, whose "Hallelujah Chorus" in the *Messiah,* is, according to White, "one of the most thrilling and effective parts ever written for the kettle drum"[14] because of its roaring crescendo.

In a modern orchestra, the timpani player, or timpanist, plays three drums whose heads measure twenty-four, twenty-six, and twenty-nine and one-half inches across. The drums have pedals that allow the tones to change with the music. The drums are struck with timpani sticks—about fourteen inches long with wooden, leather, cork, or hard felt balls on the end. Many professional players make their own timpani sticks.

Jazzing Up Drum Sets

Until the twentieth century, drums were mostly used for religious and ceremonial purposes in their lands of origin or, in the case of the timpani, to accompany classical music in the West. All that changed with the invention of jazz music in New Orleans around the end of the nineteenth century. The first jazz musicians were African Americans who blended the music of ragtime, marching bands, and blues into an entirely new musical style.

Jazz has always been rhythm based, and the first jazz bands had two drummers. One played a snare drum—a round, double-head drum, with a strand of wire, silk, or animal sinew stretched

Timpani are struck with long wooden sticks with felt, wooden, leather, or cork balls on the end.

across the bottom head. (When struck on top, the snare gives a sustained rattle, or "sizzle" sound.) The other drummer in a jazz band played a big bass drum and cymbal. The bass drum is a two-head instrument whose playing surfaces are held perpendicular to the ground so the drummer can use mallets in both hands to pound out a beat on both heads.

Since most jazz musicians were poor, drummers could not afford fancy equipment and were often forced to improvise drum kits to keep up with the everchanging styles of music. These players put together a "kit" with a snare drum, several small bass drums called tom-toms (cylindrical single- or double-head drums), and a few cymbals. As Hart writes, "Drummers began ransacking the percussive inventory . . . [taking] elements from all over the planet—snares and bass drums from Europe, the tom-tom from China, cymbals from Turkey—and along with such homely additions as cowbells, anvils, and woodblocks invented a new kind of drumming and, incidentally, a new instrument."[15]

The drum kit was again transformed around 1920, when jazz drummer Warren "Baby" Dodds added a bass drum that could be struck with a foot pedal, a concept now universally accepted by drummers across the globe. At that time, Zildjian, a Turkish cymbal maker who had been in business for almost five hundred years, began selling their instruments throughout the United States. Drummers could now easily purchase what are known as crash and sizzle cymbals (for their tone) and ride cymbals (for the way they are continually tapped, or ridden). Finally, innovative drummer Vic Berton added two small cymbals, about thirteen inches across, to a pedal-operated stand, or "high hat," and the modern drum kit was complete.

With the drum kit in place, drummers such as Gene Krupa, Buddy Rich, Chick Webb, and dozens of others helped make jazz—and jazz drumming—world famous. Less than half a century after the first jazz drummers held down the beat with crude bass and snare drums, technically proficient jazz drummers used updated kits to execute complex rhythmic beats.

The Next Generation

Like jazz, rock music was invented by African Americans who combined several musical styles for an entirely new sound—in this case, country music, blues, and rhythm and blues. Early rock drummers often used jazz kits, but it was there that the similarities ended. The technical wizardry of jazz drummers was unnecessary for a musical style that often relied on a steady 4/4 time—that is, four beats per measure.

Despite their simplicity, drums were—and are—the heart of rock music. As rock became more sophisticated in the 1960s, the percussive instruments that drummers used had few restraints. The Grateful Dead was the first major rock band to use two

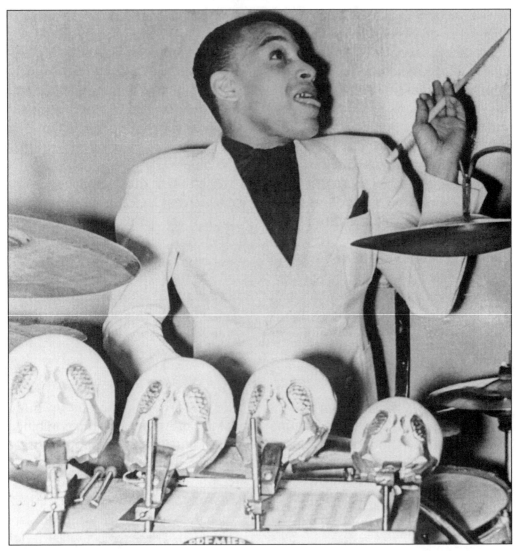

Chick Webb played complex arrangements using a drum kit and helped popularize jazz drumming.

drummers—Mickey Hart and Billy Kreutzman—and between them they loaded up the stage each night with several hundred percussive instruments including gongs, chimes, shakers, rattles, and drums from Africa, India, Cuba, China, Brazil, and elsewhere.

While rock drummers innovated, electrical engineers applied cutting-edge digital technology to one of the world's most ancient instruments. In 1983 Hans Nordelius and Mikael Carlsson invented the "Digital Percussion Plate" in a basement in Stockholm, Sweden. The instrument was known as the Clavia DMI and enabled drummers to hit the rubber disc on top of the small box and elicit sampled drum sounds, which were played through an amplifier. By 1984, the ddrumRack, with eight separate rack-mounted pads, was being sold by Clavia as demand for digital drums grew. As computer chips improved, digital drums became more realistic sounding, more complex, and more popular. They featured multisampled sounds, digital sampling options, and a vast array of rhythmic possibilities.

Whether their sound comes from a high-tech drum machine or an ancient gong cast in the tenth century, percussion instruments have bent and shaped the sound of music since humans first walked the earth. From the spiritual beat to the physical dance, every society has had a special place for percussive instruments. As Hart writes:

> You might say drums have two voices. One is technical, having to do with the drum's shape, the material it's made of, its cultural context, and the standard way it's played. Technique gives you this voice—the drum's sweet spot. . . . But once you do, the potential arises for contacting the drum's second voice—one I have come to think of as the spirit side of the drum.[16]

Chapter Two

Woodwinds

The deep, pounding rhythm of the drum and the lilting, melodious sound of the flute inhabit opposite ends of the musical spectrum. Both instruments, however, have similar roots in the distant past, and both have been utilized by cultures all over the world for religious, martial, and musical purposes.

The flute is the oldest member of the woodwind family, which includes the recorder, clarinet, oboe, bassoon, and saxophone. Woodwinds are so called because they were originally made from wood, although today some woodwinds, like the flute, are made from silver, and the saxophone is made from brass.

Woodwinds are classified as aerophones because they produce sound when a player blows air into them. The air makes a tone because it is split by the sharp edge of the mouthpiece on a flute, by one reed on a clarinet and saxophone, and by two reeds on an oboe and bassoon. The reed is made from a small piece of reed cane fixed to the mouthpiece of the instrument.

While percussion instruments are struck, and string instruments are plucked or bowed, woodwinds produce sound when a column of air vibrates in the hollow body of the instrument. Musical pitch is determined by how many holes in the instrument are covered by fingers or mechanical keys. The more holes that are covered, the longer the tube of the instrument and the lower the note. It takes practice and skill to coordinate the fingers and lips so that sounds emanate from the woodwind, but many musicians feel that the resulting music is worth the effort.

The Ancient Flute

Prehistoric wind instruments were whistles and flutes made from natural materials such as animal bone, shell, wood, or stone. These materials needed to be drilled and shaped into musical instruments, but as Raymond Meylan writes in *The Flute,* "the means of producing sound have remained virtually unchanged to this day. Nothing essentially new has appeared since antiquity, which suggests that the most important discoveries in this area were made in prehistoric times."[17]

Musical historians believe that bone whistles dating back about ten thousand years are some of the oldest flutes ever made. These instruments, found in Europe, China, South America, India, and Mesopotamia, were made simply from the toe bones of small animals and had single holes drilled through them. For example, ancient

This clay figure from ancient China holds a simple flute.

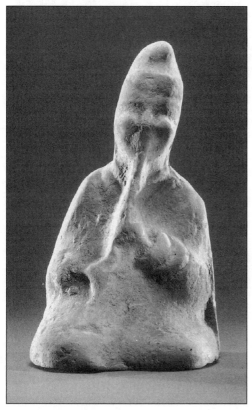

bone whistles found in caves in Switzerland were made from the toes of reindeer and small rodents known as voles. These whistles produce notes that are extremely high in pitch and barely audible to the human ear, leading researchers to believe that hunters originally used them as animal calls.

Around 3000 B.C., people living in Mesopotamia and Egypt played vertical flutes called *nay.* They were simply reed tubes that were cut at short lengths. The player held the tube below the lower lip and blew onto the edge, like blowing over the top of a bottle. The shorter the tube, the higher the pitch. Flutes similar to the nay continue to be played today in Asia and in the African countries of Cameroon and Madagascar.

Several nay of various lengths that are joined together with twine resemble the modern panpipe, whose rich, earthy tones provide a hauntingly beautiful sound. Panpipes are believed to have been invented by Chinese emperor Chuon around 2225 B.C. By the time the instrument reached Greece some sixteen hundred years later, it was known as the *syrinx.* Panpipes are still popular in northern Italy, Asia, and some South American countries.

Another primitive woodwind is the oblique flute, a tube about five feet in length, held to the side and behind the musician's body, and played with the head turned. Ancient Egyptian paintings show people playing the oblique flute. This instrument is still found in Indonesia, Iran, South America, and the Balkan countries, where it is known as

A finger-snapping singer is accompanied by a musician playing an oblique flute in this ancient Egyptian painting.

a *kaval.* The bright, cutting tone of the kaval resembles the song of an excited bird flitting through the trees.

Silver flutes, like those used in modern symphony orchestras, are based on the oblique flute design, though shorter in length. Known as transverse flutes, because the blown air passes across the mouthpiece, or embouchure, the instrument is held parallel to the ground, at a right angle from the player's face. The finger holes or keys in the flute are opened or closed to regulate the amount of air passing through the instrument's body and thus the note played.

European Development

The transverse flute seems to have moved west by the tenth century to Constantinople, Turkey (present-day Istanbul), the capital of the Byzantine Empire. In the twelfth century, the flute appeared in hand-painted books in French and German monasteries. The flutes, however, were not appreciated for their beautiful music. Instead, as Meylan writes: "They often only serve to illustrate a legend or tradition. . . . [Some images] show [flute] music as an attribute of the sirens (birds with human heads) who enchant seafarers, thereby symbolizing the dangers of the world of the senses for the Christian soul."[18]

Despite these warnings, the fife, a small, high-pitched transverse flute, was very popular in Germany, where it was played to the accompaniment of the drum for military and entertainment purposes.

Flutes Across the Globe

Flutes are universal to almost all cultures on the planet, as renowned flautist James Galway writes in Flute:

There is hardly a people in the world today, primitive or developed, that doesn't play some sort of flute. End-blown flutes range from six-foot monsters in New Guinea to the "Bushman's flute" in Africa, made from an ostrich quill. Flageolets [small end-blown flutes] are found in one form or another pretty well everywhere. In Java they have one called the *suling* which is played with their famous . . . percussion bands. The North American Indians have the Apache flute, a rather cumbrous instrument nicknamed the "lover's flute." We have our own folk flageolet, too. When I played one as a kid it was called a penny whistle. . . .

India and Japan are great flute-playing countries. The Hindus' god Krishna is often represented playing a transverse flute with finger holes, known as a *murli*. The name *bansari* is given to several kinds of flute. Originally it meant one made of bamboo (*banse* means bamboo), a simple instrument with a range of under two octaves, some end-blown but some, like the *murli*, side-blown. Nowadays the *bansari* has gone up in the world, and many are made of metal. You can hear them in Indian classical music and in the film music that is so popular all over India.

Japanese classical music, like so much of Japanese art, is closely bound up with tradition. The court orchestras that play the *gagaku* ("elegant music") for the *bunraku* dances have two kinds of flute, the *hichiriki*, a flageolet with nine holes, and a transverse flute. By tradition the "left-hand music" has a flute with seven holes and the "right-hand music" one with six holes.

The most common woodwinds found outside of the army and the church were wooden recorders. These instruments are end-blown flutes with a whistle-like mouthpiece that splits the air and directs it into a narrow, tubular wooden body. The recorder has seven finger holes and one thumb hole, allowing musicians to cover holes in order to play lower notes.

By the time of the Renaissance in the fifteenth century, recorders were extremely popular and played by kings and peasants alike. Groups of instruments were known as "consorts," and a recorder consort consisted of midrange

This fifteenth-century image depicts musical angels playing the recorder and trumpet.

treble recorders, two types of higher-pitch recorders called soprano and sopranino, and lower-pitch tenor recorders that played bass. With this wide range of instruments, recorder groups imitated the vocal harmony parts of church choirs.

Recorders were so popular that they eclipsed the transverse flute until 1599, when Thomas Morley, a leading English composer, wrote the first Western music for flutes. This was also the first music written for "broken consorts," groupings of several instruments rather than the same instrument of different musical ranges. Morley's composition, *Consort Lessons,* was written to be a fun—and challenging—piece for two viols, a three-lute consort, and a flute. In *Flute,* James Galway explains why the recorder was replaced by the flute:

> A recorder player can be a superlative musician, his intonation absolutely spot on, his music phrased with elegance and eloquence, but he cannot add to his instrument's capacity for simple utterance [of sound]. In contrast the flute has a range of interesting, attractive colours, powerful dynamics, and a compass extending from an ominous hollow sound at the bottom to a fierce cutting edge at the top. . . . [The] flute is capable of great expressiveness, but—and here comes the crunch—its expressiveness depends entirely on the skill of the player.

With the help of a skilled player or two, the flute's wider resources and greater expressiveness finally won it acceptance as an orchestral and solo instrument.[19]

Seventeenth- and eighteenth-century music for the flute was embraced by French nobility, who set fashion trends for the rest of Europe, and the instrument gained widespread popularity. These early twenty-four-inch flutes were usually made from boxwood, and skilled players could achieve a two-and-one-half octave range. (An octave consists of eight notes in the same key; for example, a C octave is C-D-E-F-G-A-B-C, with no sharp or flat notes.)

Despite their popularity, flutes were problematic for composers. The wood was affected by changes in the weather, and the instrument was often out of tune with keyboards and hence the rest of the orchestra. In 1776, Sir John Hawkins, author of the first history of music in English, wrote about the off-key intonation of the flute: "The . . . transverse flute still retains some degree of [praise] among gentlemen whose ears are not nice enough to inform them that it is never in tune."[20] In 1809, Beethoven put it more bluntly, writing to a friend, "I cannot make up my mind to write for the flute because this instrument is too limited and imperfect."[21]

The Boehm Flute

Various improvements were made to the transverse flute over the centuries to aid in the tuning and playing of the in-strument. For example, around 1670 the flute was divided into three separate pieces, known as the head, body, and foot. These sections could be adjusted by moving them slightly in or out to finely tune the instrument.

With these and other developments, the flute was improved enough so that every symphony orchestra employed up to four flautists by the eighteenth century. Beautiful and inspiring music was written for the flute by renowned composers such as Wolfgang Amadeus Mozart and Joseph Haydn. The next big change in the flute did not come until 1828, however, when Theobald Boehm opened a flute factory in Munich, Germany.

By this time the complicated instrumental and choral works of composers such as Beethoven called for a much more accurate instrument than the early-style flute. As Nancy Toff writes in *The Development of the Modern Flute:*

> The defects of the flute were . . . revealed in its growing role in the orchestra. Intonational discrepancies . . . in comparison with the highly flexible strings, were obvious. But even more important were the flute's failings with regard both to quantity and quality of sound. . . .
>
> The wooden German flute clearly could not fulfill the requirements of the nineteenth century. Its intonation was uncertain; its tone, though mellow and even beautiful in chamber music, was relatively

weak, better designed for total blending than for a solo role with the orchestra; and its dynamic capacity was not sufficient to compete with the improved brass section of the . . . orchestra.[22]

To solve these problems, Boehm began experimenting with the flute, trying to fix the age-old problems of tuning and pitch. Meylan writes that "everything was . . . called into question—profile, material and thickness of the body, the number, size and spacing of the tone-holes, and the size of the embouchure hole."[23]

Boehm constructed a flute with a complicated system of rods, levers, and keys that the player could manipulate. Instead of manually covering the instrument's holes with their fingertips, flautists could press, for example, a single key with one finger that might cover several holes. This forward leap in flute design allowed a flautist to play a three-octave range in

The modern flute descends from Theobald Boehm's flute, the first flute that used rods, levers, and keys to vary its sound.

any key with nine fingers. In *Clarinet,* Jack Bymer explains how the keys work:

> [The] function of [the keys] is effectively to vary the length of the tube. . . . The keys help the fingers close the holes, starting at the top and letting the air escape from the nearest hole below the lowest one closed. This alters the pitch of the sound produced—the longer the tube, the lower the note, in the simplest sense of instrumental acoustics.[24]

Boehm's flute quickly became the standard in orchestras throughout the world, and his mechanized system of keys and levers was soon applied to other woodwind and brass instruments.

Boehm further changed the sound of music with the invention of the solid silver flute in 1846, which yielded a clear, loud tone. Boehm describes the advantages of the silver flute:

> The superior excellence in regard to tone and intonation of my flute, made entirely of silver . . . was so striking that it was remarked by every one immediately. These metal flutes are not subject to splitting . . . and require neither to be oiled nor to be frequently played, but they always sound equally well. And even temperature affects them less than wooden flutes, because the metal, being an excellent conductor of heat, reaches its highest possible temperature in a few

seconds, so that the pitch cannot rise any higher. . . . The silver flute is preferable for playing in very large rooms because of its . . . unsurpassed brilliancy and [resonance] of its tone.[25]

While silver flutes became very popular among professionals and students alike, wooden flutes have remained in use throughout the years. Made from cocus wood from the West Indies and South America, wooden flutes deliver a dense, warm, rich sound, while those made of silver, platinum, or even gold yield a lighter, lilting sound.

Reeds and Woodwinds

Flute players split the air blown from their lips over the mouthpiece of their instrument. While difficult, the embouchure remains solid and predictable. Players of other woodwinds, however, must split the air by blowing it over a reed, which can have a positive or negative effect on the sound of the instrument. Anthony Baines explains in *Woodwind Instruments and Their History:*

> Oboists, clarinettists [*sic*], and bassoonists are entirely dependent upon a short-lived vegetable matter of merciless capriciousness, with which, however, when it behaves, are wrought perhaps the most tender and expressive sounds of all wind music. . . .

> No string player has one-tenth the trouble with his sheep's guts

Bagpipes

The bagpipe, most famously played by Scottish Highlanders, is an ancient instrument whose use has been widespread throughout Europe. The instrument consists of an airtight leather bag, which is often covered with cloth. A long melody pipe, or chanter, is fitted with a reed and contains finger holes on which melodies are played. Two other pipes, the tenor drone and bass drone, are also fitted with reeds. Finally, a fourth pipe, or blowpipe, is placed in the player's mouth so that he or she may inflate the bag with air. This is equipped with a one-way valve so air may be blown into the bag but cannot escape into the player's mouth.

A musician holds the bag under his or her left arm and inflates the bag through the blowpipe. As the bag is squeezed under the arm, the air within continually blows over the reeds in the melody and drone pipes, making music even when the musician takes breaths of air. Meanwhile the fingers of both hands open and close the holes on the melody pipe, producing a song, while the drone pipes hum in constant single notes.

This action produces loud music that can sometimes carry for miles. As such, the bagpipes have been utilized on battlefields for centuries.

This sixteenth-century illustration portrays a musician playing an early version of the bagpipe.

[strings] that the reed player has with his bits of a Mediterranean weed. For in terms of plant economy, this is all that reed cane is.[26]

Reed cane is grown in many places including Italy, Spain, and Mexico, but the finest comes from the area around Cannes, France. The process of making reeds is not automated, and artisans who specialize in making them are rare. As such, many skilled players split, cut, and shape their own reeds, hoping to obtain that ellusive and sublime sound. Whatever difficulties a reed player may encounter, musicians who play the oboe have twice as much trouble, since it is an instrument that has two reeds.

A Greek woman plays the aulos *in this image from 490 B.C.*

Roots of the Oboe

Oboes are long tubular instruments that resemble clarinets. They are made of dark tropical wood called *grenadilla.* Modern oboes have fifteen or more silver- or nickel-plated keys. The two reeds protrude from the mouthpiece, and the player produces sounds by blowing over them, causing a column of air to vibrate within the conical bore of the instrument. By manipulating the keys, the player can produce notes in more than three octaves.

Like flutes, ancestors of double-reed oboes first appeared in antiquity. The oldest oboe ever discovered was found near Ur, Mesopotamia, and is believed to have been made around 2800 B.C. After that time, oboelike instruments were common throughout the Middle East, and murals of young women playing oboes were painted in the tombs of ancient Egyptian pharaohs around 1400 B.C.

In the fifth century B.C. the Greeks called the oboe the *aulos.* Its invention was credited to Athena, the goddess of wisdom. The *aulos* is still played today and has an exotic tone that sounds like a cross between a flute and a violin. In 490 B.C., Greek musician and poet Pindar described the sound of the *aulos,* writing that it was "many voiced. . . [and imitated] a cry exceedingly shrill . . . that tune, which oft swelleth forth from the thin plate of brass, and from the reeds which grow beside the fair city of Graces."[27] Pindar's words also demonstrate the popularity of the instrument at that time—they were written for the Greek national *aulos*-playing contest, which was considered as important as the Olympic Games.

The *aulos,* like many other instruments, was also used for military purposes. Greek author Thucydides describes Spartan aulos players in battle: "The [Spartans] moved slowly and to the music of many aulos-players, who were stationed in their ranks, and played, not as an act of religion, but in order that the army might march evenly in a true measure, and that the line might not break."[28]

The Romans called the *aulos* the *tibia* and made the instruments from metal, bone, and wood. They utilized *tibia* players at gladiator games—and after the contests—at funerals.

Today, oboelike instruments that resemble the ancient *aulos* are found throughout Asia and the Middle East. In India, players of the *shahnai,* which resembles the *aulos,* may play two of the instruments at the same time. Oboes are also found in Thailand and Korea, and there are three different kinds of oboes in Southeast Asia.

In *The Oboe and the Bassoon,* Gunther Joppig describes the *hichiriki,* a member of the oboe family used in the imperial court in Japan:

In Japan the Court musicians play the *hichiriki* to this day. It is a high-pitched instrument with a piercing tone, and is used in *gagaku,* the oldest polyphonic music in existence. Nowadays the Court musicians can also play the modern oboe, and listeners at Court concerts are often surprised by the fact that, after playing a piece from the traditional repertoire, the musicians exchange the ancient instruments for modern Western ones and proceed to perform a symphony by Mozart or Beethoven.[29]

European Changes

Oboelike woodwinds seemed to have traveled the same route to Europe as drums and other musical instruments; they were brought by Arab traders by way of Constantinople in the first millennium A.D. The instrument was adapted by wandering minstrels, known as pipers, who also carried guitars, harps, and other small instruments. These minstrels played music for wealthy citizens wherever they went— even into the bath—and piped for the rich on journeys, at banquets, during church services, and before battles.

The pipers played several kinds of double-reed oboelike instruments that were known as shawms in England and *pommers* in Germany. While the instruments may have been common, according to Baines, their sound was less than enchanting: "[Of] all musical sounds that . . . day to day smote the ears of a sixteenth-century town resident, the deafening skirl [shriek] of the shawm band in palace courtyard or market square must have been the most familiar, save perhaps only for the throbbing of a lute through somebody's open window."[30]

Like the primitive flute, shawms and *pommers* were not agile enough—or suitably in tune—to play the multipart, or polyphonic, music that emerged during the Renaissance. By the seventeenth century, wind instruments had fallen out of fashion, replaced by the violin and the relatively new brass trumpet. In seventeenth-century France, however, the shawm, known as the hautbois, received a makeover by a woodwind company owned by Jean Hotteterre. The new oboe was divided into three parts: the top, bottom, and bell, and the double reed was placed directly between the lips. As Baines writes,

[The instrument builders] set about designing an improvement on [the shawm] according to their own ideas; a *new* hautbois that would be altogether more useful in the kinds of music coming into fashion. It would be flexible in dynamic range, and would possess a really good upper register—a register that had previously been badly neglected in reed instruments, but was now urgently required by the new musical styles. . . .

From the first the oboe was a success, and as it quickly became

known in other countries it seems to have impressed musicians above all through the splendid expressive range of its sound. To the trumpet were allotted airs of joyous and brilliant character; to the flutes, those of the "languishing and melancholy" kind; but the new oboe, like the human voice and the violin, could encompass every mood. In the matter of volume alone, it could be played nearly as loud as a trumpet and yet as soft as the recorder.[31]

Hotteterre's oboe was quickly picked up by musicians in royal courts across the European continent. King Louis XIV adapted it for military music where three oboes—tenor, bass, and middle—played harmonious parts along with side drums.

By the nineteenth century, the musical forces that had required changes in the construction of the flute also overtook the oboe. This was necessary, as Philip Bate writes in *The Oboe,* because composers "have always shown a tendency to write . . . beyond the capacity of their most skilled performers, who have in turn made ever-increasing demands on the instrument maker."[32]

Mechanical improvements much like those on the Boehm flute were made on the oboe, resulting in the addition of new keys that expanded the musical range of the instrument. By the early twentieth century, there were several different key configurations for the oboe, and as Bate writes: "Now it seemed for a while that the last word had indeed been spoken."[33] From its roots in ancient Egypt, the oboe had evolved into a versatile instrument with a great range and beautiful tone.

The Bassoon

Just as the oboe was derived from the shawm, instruments such as the bass *pommer* evolved into the bassoon, which is essentially a double-reed bass oboe. The wooden body of the bassoon is often made from ebony or boxwood and utilizes a long U-shaped tube divided into four parts—the wing, butt, long joint, and bell joint. The double-reed mouthpiece is attached to the body by a thin, curved metal pipe.

The instrument is meant to play in the bass register and has a range that is more than an octave lower than the oboe. Like the oboe, there are several types of bassoon that play in various ranges. For example, the contrabassoon, or double bassoon, that plays an octave below the bassoon, around the same notes as the lowest keys of a piano.

The earliest bassoonlike instruments were found in Germany in the mid-1500s and later throughout Europe. Baines describes the sound:

> With a suitably-made reed, the old "horse's leg," as people called the bassoon in England, sounds irresistibly sweet and beautiful; something like a well-played modern French bassoon, but a little softer, more firm and compact,

and rather cello-like. Like the old oboe, it blends supremely well with every other instrument, while yet it possessed sufficient weight to have been a favourite solo instrument.[34]

The construction of the modern bassoon has changed little since the 1800s.

Like other woodwinds, over the centuries instrument makers in France, Germany, and elsewhere tinkered with the bassoon, changing the key arrangements and construction materials, and adding mechanical keys in the nineteenth century. Since that time, the bassoon has changed little and, like the oboe, remains today as it was perfected in the 1800s.

The Clarinet

While the bassoon is limited to bass parts, the clarinet is one of the most diverse woodwind instruments, with a range of nearly four complete octaves. The instrument has, according to Bymer, "a subtler variety of tone quality, from velvet-soft to steely-hard—and . . . [an] ability to blend with other instruments which makes it the essential 'binding' factor of the wood-wind section."[35]

The single-reed clarinet, most often made from African blackwood, was invented rather than developed over time. The clarinet is based on a primitive reed instrument known as the *chalumeau,* described by Baines as a "little instrument less than a foot long, [that produced] . . . toy trumpet noises."[36]

Around 1700, Nuremberg instrument maker Johann Christian Denner added two keys to the *chalumeau,* which gave the instrument a range of over two octaves. Around 1716, the term "clarinette" was first used in a written advertisement for Denner's new instrument.

By filling an important role in the woodwind section, the clarinet gained

Jazz clarinetist Benny Goodman was known as the "King of Swing."

instant popularity throughout Europe in the eighteenth century. The instrument was described by Italian musician Fillipo Bonnani in 1722:

> An instrument similar to the oboe is the clarone [*sic*]. It is two and a half palms long and terminates in a bell like the trumpet three inches in width. It is pierced with seven holes in front and one behind. There are in addition two other holes opposite to each other, but not diametrically, which are closed and opened by two springs pressed by the finger.[37]

Like other woodwinds, however, the clarinet had a limited range, was not musically accurate, and was difficult to play until the Boehm mechanical-key system was added to it in 1843.

Meanwhile, composers from Mozart to Richard Wagner had been composing music for the instrument, and talented clarinetists were part of every symphony orchestra. The tone was described in the nineteenth century by author William Gardiner, who wrote that the clarinet "approaches the tone of the

The Jazz Clarinet

While woodwinds remained part of symphony orchestras, the clarinet took on a life of its own in twentieth-century jazz bands. Jazz developments and clarinet players are discussed in The Cambridge Companion to the Clarinet, *edited by Colon Lawson:*

Listen to almost any performance from the first decade of recorded jazz and you will hear the sound of the clarinet. Whether you choose to listen to the Original Dixieland Jazz Band . . . , the King Oliver/Louis Armstrong recordings or Jelly Roll Morton's Red Hot Peppers, you will hear every ensemble topped by upper-register clarinet, playing in harmony above the melody.

All the evidence about the origins of jazz points to the music having developed from vocal performances. After the end of the Civil War in 1865 the New Orleans blacks were able gradually to acquire the instruments of the military band, including the clarinet. Military (marching) bands were important in all-French settlements, and in New Orleans most of the early jazz players started their careers in such wind bands, playing marches, polkas, quadrilles and so on. From these two sources—the vocal folk/dance music and the marching band—it is quite easy to understand how the five- or six-piece jazz bands evolved. . . . [And] it is with these smaller "marching bands," with their trumpet-trombone-clarinet front line, that jazz first appeared. . . .

[During the swing era] . . . in the late 1930s . . . jazz became the pop music of the day, [it was] the age of the big swing band fronted and led by a virtuoso instrumentalist. This was the heyday of [clarinetist] Benny Goodman, the "King of Swing," and Artie Shaw, the "King of the Clarinet." . . . Goodman made his first trio recordings when he was not yet eighteen . . . [and] is the clarinettist's clarinettist.

female voice nearer than any other instrument, and as a principal in the orchestra it now sustains a distinguished part. . . . In quality of tone it is warm and powerful; partaking somewhat of the oboe and the trumpet combined, and the lustre of its tones adds great [radiance] to the orchestra."[38]

The Saxophone

The saxophone was the last woodwind to be invented. Although it is made from brass, it is classified as a woodwind because it utilizes a single reed. The alto saxophone features a ninety-degree bend after the mouthpiece and then doubles back on itself after a two-and-one-half-foot section with twenty keys. There is a flared bell at the end. The soprano saxophone, made popular by light jazz musician Kenny G, is straight and looks like a brass clarinet. Musicians play it by blowing air over the reed and manipulating the keys to produce different notes.

The saxophone was named after its Belgian inventor, Adolphe Sax, and its name means "the sound of Sax." Sax first showed his instrument to the public in 1841 at the Brussels Exhibition. Sax was a creative inventor and developed at least fourteen horns for the saxophone family, varying in size and key including E-flat sopranino, B-flat soprano, F alto, C tenor, E-flat baritone, C bass, and E-flat contrabass. Today the fourteen horns of Sax have been reduced to three standard sizes that remain in widespread use—the soprano, the tenor, and the baritone.

The sound of the saxophone was remarkable to music critics. Nineteenth-century author J.G. Kastner wrote of "the nobility and beauty of its timbre [tone color]. . . . I cannot say it enough times, the saxophone is called to the highest destiny by the beauty of its timbre and that opinion is common with several notable musicians . . . who have heard it the same time as myself. . . . [And Italian composer Gioachino Rossini wrote:] This is the most beautiful kind of sound that I have ever heard!"[39]

The new horn gained widespread publicity in 1845 when Sax proposed a "battle of the bands," highlighting his instruments in front of an audience of twenty thousand in Paris. At the contest, one band of forty-five musicians played military music on traditional instruments, while another band of the same size used an ensemble made up entirely of saxophones of various shapes and sizes. Kastner described the contest:

> Sax's large infantry band of sax-horns . . . compared favourably with the older [-style orchestra], which suffered . . . from the enormous gap in the middle harmonies, the thin cutting tone of the oboes mixing ill with the rest, the swollen-faced bassoonists with no carrying power whatever, and despite some good use of valve horns, the sterile buzzing of hand-horns in the open air, still worse on the march.[40]

The general opinion was that the saxophones blew away the competition, and the instruments' inventor was awarded a contract to supply the French military with saxophones. During the following decades, several major composers wrote works utilizing the saxophone, most notably Georges Bizet's opera *L'Arlesienne* and Maurice Ravel's famous orchestral work, *Bolero*. By the end of the twentieth century, an estimated two thousand ballets, operas, and symphonies included musical parts written for the saxophone.

Soulful Sounds

Meanwhile, the influence of French marching bands was strong in New Or-

leans around the turn of the century when African American musicians were combining military music with ragtime and blues to create the new musical style called jazz. While early jazz horn players used cornets, trombones, and clarinets, by the 1920s the saxophone had been embraced by jazz players, especially clarinetists whose instrument most resembles the saxophone.

The saxophone was perfect for this improvised style of music, since it was capable of expressing the guttural honk of the low-down blues, the smoky melancholy of slow dance music, and the soaring riffs of melodious swing tunes. By the 1930s, big band composers such as Duke Ellington

Although it is made from brass, the saxophone is considered a woodwind because it is played using a single reed.

Rockin' Saxophones

While mainly associated with jazz, saxophones were part of the rock-and-roll revolution in the 1950s and 1960s, as Richard Ingham and John Helliwell write in The Cambridge Companion to the Saxophone:

Saxophone solos in the Bill Haley band were taken by tenor player Rudy Pompelli (*Shake, Rattle and Roll,* 1954), and despite the growing domination of the (electric) guitar, the saxophone was relied on to push the excitement factor in many bands. Lee Allen featured with Little Richard and Fats Domino, King Curtis was the soloist on the Coasters' *Yakety Yak* (1958) and Charlie Brown (1959), and Ray Charles used Hank Crawford for many years. . . .

The early 1960s produced two novelty numbers which were none the less influential in their own way, Boots Randolph's *Yakkety Sax* (1963) and Henry Mancini's classic *Pink Panther* . . . in 1964. The decade as a whole produced the great solo artistry of King Curtis and Junior Walker on the one hand, and the soul horn sections of James Brown and the Motown groups on the other. Junior Walker and King Curtis, both tenor players, were enormously influential and enjoyed great commercial success. They defined the rock tenor sound of the 1960s, with extraordinary control of high tones, flutter-tonguing, growls, shakes and, above all, sensitive phrasing. . . . Walker was a singer as well as a saxophonist—his hits included *Shotgun* (1965) and *How Sweet It Is* (1966). . . . The horn section developed in this decade into a regular feature, particularly with the Motown vocal groups. . . . The horns were a vital part of the James Brown sound, from *Out of Sight* (1964), the beginnings of funk, through *Cold Sweat* (1967) and into the 1970s.

The end of the 1960s saw jazz embracing rock in the work of Miles Davis and others; in the band Blood, Sweat and Tears . . . known as a rock "big band," one of [their] most notable recordings was *Spinning Wheel*. . . . The successful band Chicago included Walter Parazaider on saxophone. These groundbreaking ventures also seemed to give legitimacy to the idea of jazz artists being used as session players for rock and pop recordings.

Innovative saxophonist Charlie Parker specialized in bebop jazz.

and melodies. In the sixties, players such as John Coltrane (tenor and soprano sax) went beyond bebop to free-form jazz, wringing improvised sounds from the saxophone no one had previously believed were humanly possible.

The Woodwind Section

The woodwinds have played an important role in classical music since the Middle Ages. Most symphony orchestras employ four flutes, four oboes, and a pair of bassoons. After the invention of the clarinet, orchestras utilized four clarinetists as well. Since they were invented in 1840, few classical composers wrote music for saxophones. As a result, most orchestras do not have a saxophone section, but sometimes clarinetists double as sax players.

The music of the woodwinds can be described as organic, adding the music of nature—and human breath—to the orchestra. Galway sums up this feeling in the following passage, written about the flute, but appropriate for other woodwinds:

> The sound comes from inside the body, in a way not possible with instruments to be hit or scraped. It is an extension of the player's speaking and singing voice. His breath, his muscles, his fingers produce the sound, without intervening technical complications. Nothing separates him from the tone, no mechanism, . . . no hammer, no bow nor string. Only singers have less paraphernalia between them and their listeners.[41]

were filling out their orchestras with five saxophone players—two altos, two tenors, and a baritone. These saxophone sections contained numerous talented soloists such as Illinois Jacquet and Buddy Tate, who became minor stars in their own right.

Louis Jordan, who sang, composed, and played the alto sax, developed the fast-paced, "jump blues" sound, writing songs in the 1940s—such as the rollicking "Caledonia"—that were the forerunners of rock and roll.

During the fifties, players such as Charlie Parker (alto sax) revolutionized jazz—and the way the saxophone was played. Parker specialized in bebop—manic music with complex harmonies

Chapter Three

Brass

In the era before microphones and amplifiers, brass instruments created the loudest sounds emanating from any orchestra. Their attention-attracting reverberations were utilized by kings in their royal courts and were essential to generals on the battlefield.

Even today, few unamplified instruments can surpass the volume, brightness, and resonance of a well-played trumpet, tuba, or trombone. Whether performing a delicate passage written by Beethoven or marching across a football field blaring "Louie Louie," brass sections hold a unique place in musical history, having been utilized for nearly every style of music from classical to rock and roll. As stated in *The Cambridge Companion to Brass Instruments:*

> There is probably no other family of instruments which has been more affected by the progress of history, with its attendant social changes, technical inventions and musical fashions. These changes have resulted in each instrument having not one, but several idioms. Such diversities are exemplified by the . . . modern performer who, on any day of the week, may be required to imitate the style of the seventeenth century, the nineteenth century, 1920s Broadway, modern jazz . . . or play the music of their own time within the current parameters of taste and style.[42]

Vibrating Sound Waves

Like woodwinds, brass instruments such as trumpets, tubas, and French horns are aerophones, but differ from flutes, oboes, clarinets, and bassoons in how they are played. Instead of a column of air vibrating within the instrument, as happens with woodwinds, brass instruments amplify the vibrations caused by the musician's lips. This is facilitated by the mouthpiece, upon which the player makes an airtight seal with his or her lips. This process is explained by Arnold Myers in *The Cambridge Companion to Brass Instruments:*

> The column of air inside the tube is set into vibration when it is excited by the player buzzing his/her lips placed against the mouthpiece. A sustained sound on brass instruments requires . . . sound waves travelling from one end to the other and reflected from each end like water waves in a bath. . . . Whether the other end of the instrument terminates abruptly (as in

a bugle) or terminates with a flaring bell (as in a trumpet), sound waves are reflected by the bell mouth or by the flare."[43]

When the air within the brass tube starts vibrating, the tiny particles form fast-moving wave patterns that vibrate back and forth. By blowing harder or softer, the player can change the wave pattern to produce different notes. For example, by blowing with relaxed lips, a trumpet player can play the lowest note on his instrument—called the fundamental note. By tightening the lips and blowing harder, the player may produce a sound eight notes—or an oc-

Musicians create sound from brass instruments by blowing air into a mouthpiece. The air then vibrates to produce different tones.

tave—higher than the fundamental note. This is called the first overtone. By blowing harder still—and with tighter lips—the player produces a pitch that is one octave plus five notes higher, called the second overtone. This process can be completed to produce notes in what are known as an overtone series.

The overtones emanating from the instrument may be changed by valves moved up and down by the fingers, as in a trumpet or tuba, or by a long sliding tube as in a trombone.

Before valves were invented, trumpet players could only play the notes in these overtone series, but not scales or melodies. As such, bugle players, whose instruments do not have valves, can play only five notes. They perform simple songs such as "Taps" or "Reveille" by changing the vibrations of their lips to change pitch.

Making Brass Instruments

The general consensus among brass players is that the quality of their playing is affected by the materials and craft work utilized in the construction of their instruments.

Brass is an alloy metal composed of about 70 percent copper and 30 percent zinc. The natural trumpet of the Renaissance era was made from fourteen separate pieces of brass. The bell, tubing, saddles, and other pieces were made from sheet brass that was wrapped into various shaped tubes. The seams were then sealed with an alloy solder. The brass, however, often became hard and brittle when it was bent, hammered, and stretched. To keep the metal soft, it had to be heated to a red-hot temperature and then cooled. This blackened the surface of the metal with an oxide layer that later had to be removed by what was known as "pickling" in a bath of acid.

Before this was done, however, the bell was formed by heating, cooling, and hammering. Finally the instrument was burnished, or finely shaped, on a metal rod called a mandrel, sanded, and polished to a fine finish.

Machinery has taken over much of the work of making modern brass instruments. The sheet metal is cut and formed by machines, which are run by highly skilled workers. The bell is formed on an electric lathe that spins the metal at a high speed while it is shaped by a worker using wooden "shaping wands," knives, and other tools.

To bend the tubing, liquid lead is poured into the tube and allowed to cool. The tube may then be bent by hand without collapsing or cracking. Once it is finished, the tube is heated and the lead is poured out. Cheaper instruments are bent by machines.

The bell is soldered to the tubing, and more than 150 parts come together to make a modern instrument such as a trumpet. Valves must be made with space-age accuracy, with the pistons that move up and down inside the mechanism set at no more than one ten-thousandth of an inch from the valve wall.

The Historical Trumpet

While modern technicians can turn out a new trumpet in less than six hours, the origins of the instrument are as old as humankind itself. Musicologists believe that the first trumpet may have been a tree branch made hollow by rot or insects. Unlike modern trumpets, these ancient instruments had no mouthpiece and no flared bell. They were not even used to make music, but rather utilized as megaphones to amplify a person's voice so that it could be heard at great distances. Shamans used this distorted noise to gain the attention of the gods or to ward off evil spirits, as Edward Tarr writes in *The Trumpet*:

> Such megaphone trumpets were sounded at religious and magical rites: circumcisions, burials and sunset ceremonies. They were played only by men and were thus identified with the male sex, as opposed to certain drum forms which were supposed to be feminine. Trumpets such as these can still be found in the primitive cultures of New Guinea and northwest Brazil, as well as in the form of the Australian didjeridu.[44]

Later trumpets with a more refined sound may have been made from animal horns, elephant tusks, large seashells, or even human thighbones.

In ancient Egypt, trumpets, like so many other musical instruments, were used for military and religious purposes. Its invention was credited to

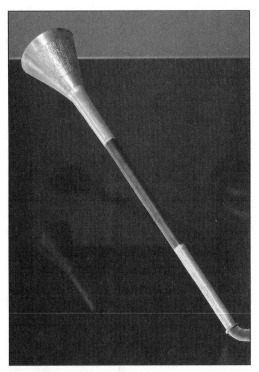

In ancient Egypt, trumpets, such as this one, served a military or religious purpose.

Osiris, the god of the underworld, but again, the trumpet was not used to play enjoyable music. In fact, according to Tarr, the Greek author Plutarch "compared the sound of the Egyptian trumpet with the braying of [a donkey]."[45] Despite the musical criticism, these trumpets, about twenty inches long, were made from hammered silver or bronze, and were extremely valuable.

Trumpets made from silver are also mentioned prominently in the Bible. In the Book of Numbers, God tells Moses: "And when you go to war in your land against the adversary who oppresses you, then you shall sound the alarm with trumpets . . . and you should be saved from your enemies. On the day after gladness also, and reported feasts, at the beginnings of your months, you should blow the trumpets." The ancient Israelites also used a trumpet made from a ram's horn called a shofar, which is still blown today on Jewish holidays.

The ancient Greek trumpet, known as the *salphinx,* was sectional, was made from straight tubing over five feet long, had more than a dozen sections

Indian and Asian Trumpets

In The Trumpet, *Edward Tarr writes about trumpets used in Indian and Asian countries:*

The South Indian trumpet, called tirucinnam . . . was similar to the . . . Egyptian trumpet. It was about [thirty inches] long, had a wide cylindrical bore, and a narrow, conical bell, but no mouthpiece. The reason for the lack of mouthpiece is clear; the tirucinnam player always blew two of these instruments simultaneously.

Another kind of Indian trumpet, the end-blown shell trumpet called sankha . . . is mentioned here . . . because of its exclusively religious use. On the last day of the earth, when everything goes up in flames, the god Siva will play the shell trumpet—as will the seven angels of the biblical Last Judgement.

The modern North Indian trumpet seems to be derived from central Asiatic and Far Eastern trumpets or at least to be related to them.

Like the Chinese trumpet, it is narrow and conical and consists of four telescoping sections, the ends of which are each provided with a kind of knob. Besides the end-blown shell trumpet (hai lo in Chinese, hora in Japanese), which is played by sailors and Buddhist priests, there was also in China a very long cylindrical metal trumpet (hao t'ung in Chinese, dokaku in Japanese), the bell end of which rests on the ground while the instrument is being played. . . . The hao t'ung was played at burials. . . .

The Tibetan trumpet, called dung, can be as long as nearly [sixteen feet in length]. It is made of copper, has a conical bore, and also consists of several telescoping sections with knobs. When it is blown during lama rites, it usually rests on the ground. Like many Asiatic trumpet instruments related to it, the dung has a broad, very flat mouthpiece. Only low, roaring tones are played on it.

made from ivory, and was held together with bronze rings. The mouthpiece and flared end, or bell, were made from cast bronze, and the tone was described by one ancient poet as "screaming."[46]

The Romans called their trumpet a tuba, although it little resembled a modern tuba. Used by soldiers on the march, this instrument was about four feet long and made from a straight tube with a bell on the end. The Romans also had a type of trumpet known as a *lituus,* a J-shaped shrieking instrument used to frighten the enemy in war.

Improving the Trumpet

By the Middle Ages, trumpets were widely used across Europe. At that time, kings, princes, knights, and other nobility employed wandering minstrels who played two- to six-foot-long trumpets at coronations, weddings, banquets, jousting matches, ceremonies, and festivals. Trumpeters playing on the long horns announced the arrival of aristocrats at public events. German soldiers guarding towns from towers used *thurmers,* or tower trumpeters, to blare a warning when enemies were approaching.

By this time, the nearly universal word for the instrument was found in several European languages. To the French it was the *trompe,* or *trompette;* in German, *trumpa* or *trompete;* in English, trumpet. The English also referred to trumpetlike instruments as *claro* or clarion, meaning "bright" or "clear," words that help explain the sound of the instruments.

The European trumpets were improved by new innovations in metalwork, as Keith Polk explains in *The Cambridge Companion to Brass Instruments:* "[Instruments] were available fabricated in 'S' shapes by the late fourteenth century, and in the standard 'folded' form by shortly after 1400. Once the bent forms were developed they soon took over. Straight instruments continued to be made but for most purposes players prefer the portability and control afforded by the new shapes."[47] These folded, or "natural," trumpets were about three-and-one-half feet long, made with tubing about one-half inch wide, and held a four-inch bell at one end. They were pitched to play either in the key of C or D, and could play very high notes.

The new accuracy of metalworking also allowed for the development of a new kind of instrument, the slide trumpet. This instrument was composed of a mouthpiece and a straight tube about one foot long, over which another foot-long tube with a bell slid back and forth. When the bell piece was slid out, it lowered the note; when it was pulled toward the player, it shortened the tube, thus raising the note.

The Musical Trumpet

At this point, the natural trumpet continued to be used in royal courts or on the battlefield, while the slide trumpet could be played with woodwinds and other instruments, as described by Tarr: "[Trumpeters played] in the so-called 'alta' ensemble, consisting of loud instruments . . . such as shawms (double-reed woodwind instruments) and trumpets, as opposed to the soft instruments such as . . . lutes."[48]

By the late fifteenth century, the Renaissance was changing art and music across Europe. Alta ensembles with several styles of trumpet were extremely popular in Italy, Spain, and Portugal. And in Germany, the tower trumpeters now did more than merely sound the alarm. As many as five such musicians played trumpets twice daily. From a sixteenth-century book called *The Tower Players' and Trumpeters' Oath*, trumpeters were ordered to "play five entire compositions of proper length, both in the evening . . . and in the morning at daybreak. And this shall be done from both sides of the tower."[49]

These municipal trumpeters played in five-part harmony in which every musician played in a different range. They also performed in orchestras with as many as ten players, playing bass, middle, and high parts. These groups not only performed at local dances but also played the most advanced classical music of the day. As Polk writes:

During the Renaissance, tower trumpeters played musical compositions in five-part harmony at sunrise and sunset.

[Trumpet] players were capable of performing in a variety of [counterpoint] styles, and . . . demands on their memory capacity were considerable. That is, their "unwritten" performances were probably a mixture of improvisations based on secular and sacred . . . melodies, and of repertoires of composed pieces, sacred and secular, in the most demanding styles of the day. . . . Once restricted to the marginal role of ritual, these musicians were now assuming a central role in the art music of their time.[50]

By the eighteenth century, composers such as Bach and Handel were writing music for the natural trumpet. The part for the highest register was called the *clarino;* the part beneath it was the second *clarino.* Below that came the *trompa* part—about the range of the modern trumpet. The lowest parts were played on a seven-foot-long trumpet known as the *principale.*

During the classical period of the late eighteenth century, the *clarino* fell from fashion. Composers such as Mozart and Beethoven wrote only simple parts for the horns to back up the flowing melodies of the violins and woodwinds. Distraught trumpeters and brass makers began to search for new ways to improve the instrument in order to create a demand. In 1818, two musicians, Heinrich Stölzel of the Royal Opera Orchestra of Berlin and Friedrich Blühmel, an amateur oboist, changed the instrument forever when they invented a trumpet with two valves. Valves allowed the musician to play the chromatic scale—that is, all notes within its range including sharps and flats.

The patent for valves was sold to a German instrument company, and soon trumpet players from Russia to England were picking up the valve trumpet. By 1826 a third valve had been added.

Meanwhile, composers began writing for the valve trumpet. In 1835, the opera *La Juive* by Jacques Halévy was the first to feature the instrument. Since that time, the valve trumpet has been used in classical, ragtime, jazz, rock and roll, and every other musical style, although the basic instrument has changed little since the 1820s.

A Family of Trumpets

Trumpets are made in many different sizes and shapes. Because of the length of the tube in a basic trumpet, the instrument is tuned to play in the key of B-flat. Trumpets that are slightly shorter play in the key of C, D, E, or even higher. These smaller trumpets are used to play the high *clarino* parts written by Bach and others. The piccolo trumpet is very small—half the length of the standard B-flat trumpet—and is meant to play an octave higher. On the other end of the musical scale, the bass trumpet—twice as long as the B-flat—plays an octave lower than the standard trumpet.

The cornett is a wooden horn, sort of a cross between a brass and a woodwind instrument, with six keys

Trumpets and Classical Composers

Eighteenth-century classical composers found new ways to use trumpets in their symphonies, as Edward Tarr writes in The Cambridge Companion to Brass Instruments:

Composers of the so-called Classical period, notably Joseph Haydn (1736–1809), Wolfgang Amadeus Mozart (1756–91) and Ludwig van Beethoven (1770–1827), created music in which trumpets had an entirely new function, rhythmically rather than melodically oriented. Strings and woodwind instruments, even horns (which were generally written for in pairs, sometimes in two different pitches), were more capable than the heroic trumpet of expressing the wide range of emotions which the new style demanded. Trumpets were deployed mainly as a pair, and were generally used to accentuate the [basic] tonality of a given movement or work. . . . Since their parts no longer fulfilled an easily discernible melodic function, trumpeters had to employ considerable insight and keep their ears open in order to bring their instruments into proper balance with the rest of the orchestra.

In some of his sacred music, Mozart followed the old Austrian tradition of writing for four trumpets, two high and two low. . . . Although, according to an old anecdote involving a family friend . . . Mozart had an inborn antipathy to the trumpet, he nevertheless wrote a trumpet concerto (now lost) in his early years and used the instrument tellingly in his scores.

Up to 1775, Haydn used trumpets in pairs and pitched only in C; he then gradually added the pitches of D (1775), Bb (1778–9) and Eb (in England, 1793). The Nelson Mass (1798) uses three in C.

Beethoven also adhered to the standard Classical trumpet range, writing for pairs of trumpets in Bb, C, D, Eb and F, but made new demands on endurance.

and a cup mouthpiece. The sound is produced by the player's vibrating lips, but this is modified by holes placed, like a flute, along the length of the instrument.

These instruments were originally made from animal horns more than fifteen centuries ago and are still played in rural areas of Scandinavia where bull or goat horns are used to make primitive cornetts. During the Renaissance, cornetts were very popular because their sound resembled a human voice. As Bruce Dickey writes in *The Cambridge Companion to Brass Instruments*:

> By the mid sixteenth century cornettes appeared in a rich variety of ensembles and settings from cathedrals to princely chambers, from public piazzas to court chapels. Moreover, their popularity spread to every part of Europe, undoubtedly fostered by the performances of virtuosi [talented musicians] travelling in the retinues of emperors and princes. . . .
>
> Their duties [of the musicians] were precisely spelled out: daily performances in the public square, accompanying the entrances and exits of prominent officials as well as providing entertainment for their meals, playing for processions and at public celebrations, etc.[51]

Bugles—that is, short trumpets without valves—also date back to antiquity, and the first ones were probably made from bull horns. In fact, their name comes from *bugle,* an old French word meaning "young bull." Bugles, or buglehorns, became popular with nobility during the Middle Ages and were used for hunting calls and military signals. With the advent of metalworking technology in the seventeenth century, bugle makers began to form the instruments from copper or brass. At this time they were used by town watchmen,

Brass musician Louis Armstrong was an influential figure in the history of jazz.

Louis Armstrong's Swingin' Jazz

On the "Daniel Louis 'Satchmo' 'Pops' Armstrong," website, Chris M. Slawecki writes about the trumpet talents and the musical legend that was Louis Armstrong.

Louis Armstrong is indisputably the single most important figure in the early history of jazz. As a trumpet player, Armstrong's legendary tone, exuberance, stamina and ferocity of attack remain for the most part unsurpassed; his trumpet prowess is believed by many to have single-handedly transformed jazz from an ensemble to a soloist's art form. . . .

Armstrong grew up in a waif's [orphan's] home in New Orleans, where he was exposed to the trumpet and cornet. Around 1917 he replaced his friend and early mentor King Oliver on cornet in New Orleans jazz bands led by Kid Ory, and by 1923 was in Chicago in Oliver's Creole Jazz band, as second cornet before switching to trumpet.

Playing with Oliver . . . Armstrong began to develop simply awesome chops. He made his first recordings around 1923 as Oliver's sideman; enticed with the featured trumpet [position], he joined Fletcher Henderson's New York City orchestra in 1924 and seemed to grow even stronger. As a soloist, Armstrong had already changed the course of jazz by the time he returned to Chicago in late 1925, yet his best work was still to come.

Between 1925 and 1928, Armstrong, this time out in front, recorded about sixty sides with his "Hot Five" and "Hot Seven" ensembles which endure as the single most important catalog in the entire jazz [collection]. . . . Armstrong seemed to scale musical summit after summit. By the time he recorded the majestic "West End Blues" in 1928, Armstrong had graduated from being influential to being immortal. . . .

Even as his spectacular excursions into the stratosphere of the trumpet seemed to grow more infrequent as he aged, his worldwide reputation as "The Ambassador of Jazz" kept growing until he passed away in his sleep in 1971.

stagecoach drivers, and deliverymen to announce the arrival of the mail. The modern bugle, at four feet in length, took its present form around 1800 and has changed little since then.

Although the bugle has remained the same, around 1830 an anonymous Vienna instrument maker invented the valve bugle that was named flügelhorn for the instrument blown by the *flügelmeister,* an official that presided over German hunting expeditions. Shorter and fatter than a regular trumpet, the flügelhorn is about the same length.

Flügelhorns, with their full, sensuous, and subtle tone, are not often used in classical music where the clear, clean, bright sound of the trumpet is preferred. With its rich, dark sound, however, the flügelhorn was adopted by twentieth-century jazz trumpet players such as Chet Baker and, most notably, Miles Davis. Today many jazz trumpeters also play the flügelhorn.

Like the flügelhorn, the cornet (not to be confused with the cornett) is a type of keyed bugle, although one that was very popular in nineteenth-century Europe. With a bright, brassy tone, cornets were popular in theater, orchestra, and military marching bands. Like the flügelhorn, the cornet was adapted by jazz players, particularly Louis Armstrong.

The Trombone

An instrument that evolved from the trumpet, but is not in the same fam-

The military has historically used the cornet in its marching bands.

ily, is the trombone, which has a wider—and much lower—range than the B-flat trumpet. The name itself is composed of two Italian words: *trompe,* or "trumpet," and *one,* or "big." In England, it was known by the curious term sackbut, which is actually based on the German word *sacabuche,* or "draw-pipe."

Trombones have a cup-shaped mouthpiece and a U-shaped slide mechanism. With a narrow bell, the instrument has a mellower tone than a trumpet. Originating from the slide trumpet around 1400, by the 1600s the trombone was made in three basic styles—alto, tenor, and bass. Like many other brass instruments, the trombone was favored in eighteenth-century military bands as well as in church and chamber orchestras. Modern jazz groups and marching bands favor the tenor trombone.

The slide allows trombonists to play both individual notes and glissandi, or sliding tones. With the slide pulled in, the trombone plays in a low B-flat key. As the slide is opened, the tube of the instrument is lengthened and the pitch lowers.

Unlike early unvalved trumpets, the trombone could play the entire chromatic scale. As such, composers favored trombones over trumpets and wrote music for them in opera scores. The 1787 opera *Don Giovanni* by Mozart features one of the earliest orchestral compositions for trombone. Beethoven's Fifth Symphony is notable for establishing the trombone's place in the symphony orchestra.

The French Horn

The French horn, with its funnel-like mouthpiece, wide, circular tubing, and large flared bell, was developed around the mid–seventeenth century. Its tone has been described as "velvet," meaning that it has a mellower, richer sound than horns in the trumpet family. It was not always this way, however. The French horn was developed around 1650, not surprisingly, in France. At the time it was called the *cor de chass,* roughly "horn of the chase," and used to call people from afar while hunting. This blaring horn was considered too raucous to be included in the orchestra with the subtle flutes and violins, and made an appearance on the opera stage only as a "special effects" instrument during theatrical scenes depicting a hunt.

In Germany and Austria, however, the horn was a favorite of Count Franz Anton von Sporck, who was a music lover as well as an avid hunter. The count ordered several of his musicians to learn the instrument and utilize it in classical music compositions. By the 1700s, composers began composing specifically for the French horn. The most colorful parts for the horn were written in the upper, or *clarino*, range.

By the mid-1700s, musicians developed the "hand horn" technique for the French horn, in which the player inserted the right hand into the bell. By moving the hand back and forth, players were able to play notes other than the fundamental tone and the overtones, thus filling in the previously missing notes in the chromatic scale. By the end of the century, the orchestral horn, as it was now called, became a necessary part of every orchestra. Composers such as Haydn, Mozart, and Beethoven wrote majestic solo pieces specifically for the orchestral horn.

In the 1830s, the addition of three valves, similar to those used in the trumpet, broadened the range of the

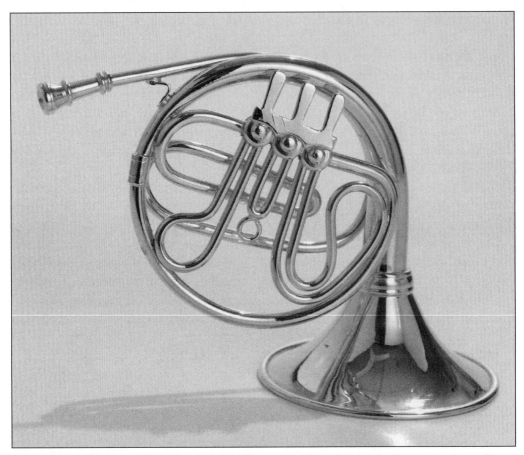

The French horn produces a rich, mellow sound and is a vital component of orchestral music.

instrument further, allowing a standard horn in the key of F to play the chromatic scale in over three octaves. Late in the nineteenth century, an additional valve was added that, when depressed, changed the entire key of the orchestral horn from F to B-flat. This four-valve instrument, known as the double horn, is widely used today and not only in classical music. The double horn may be heard on the Beatles' *Revolver* album and is occasionally used in pop and jazz music as well.

The Tuba

While the orchestral horn player reaches for the high notes, no brass player hits lower notes than the tuba player. Based on the Latin word for trumpet, the tuba was patented in 1835 by Friedrich Wilhelm Wieprecht, a Prussian bandmaster, and Johann Gottfried Moritz, a German instrument maker. The inventors based their new instrument on the valved bass bugle and an S-shaped wooden horn called a serpent.

The tuba is the largest of the brass instruments. With a wide-bore, coiled tubing, three to five valves, a deep cup-like mouthpiece, and large, upward bell, the instrument is the deep "oom-pah" bass of the orchestra or band. While able to cover a three-octave range, the F tuba can reach the second C below middle C.

The large-scale tuba with its deep bass resonance demonstrates that brass instruments have come a long way since the biblical Gabriel blew his silver horn. From the shrieking blast meant to scare the enemy on an ancient battlefield to the sublime sounds of a modern jazz quartet, brass instruments tell a story in music that is nearly as old as humanity itself.

Chapter Four

Strings

Instruments with strings, such as the guitar and violin, are some of the most popular in the world. And the family of stringed instruments, known as chordophones, have been part of human history for tens of thousands of years.

Cave paintings in France dating back nearly fifteen thousand years depict a man with what researchers believe is a one-stringed instrument being played with a bow or possibly being hit with a rhythm stick. This type of primitive instrument was probably made from animal sinew rolled tightly into a string and possibly stretched across a gourd. By 1900 B.C., ancient Babylonian paintings showed nude figures playing stringed instruments that resembled guitars. Later, in ancient Egypt, people plucked harps and lyres.

In all, the chordophone family has three branches. The first consists of instruments with a neck and includes guitars, violins, cellos, banjos, Indian sitars, and mandolins. These have strings of equal length that are of varying thickness and tension. When the strings are shortened by fingers applied to the neck of the instrument, a higher pitch results. The strings are set into vibration by strumming or plucking with fingers, picks, or bows. The second division features instruments such as the zither, dulcimer, and Japanese koto, which utilize strings stretched across a flat body.

A third branch includes plucked instruments with multiple strings, such as the lyre, where each string produces only one pitch. Harps are part of this family, which is further divided into two subcategories: the harp proper, in which the strings may be plucked by either hand from each side, and the psaltery, where the strings are stretched over a soundboard and may be played only from one side. (A soundboard is a thin sheet of wood placed under—or above—the strings to increase resonance.)

The Ancient Lyre

One of the most ancient instruments classified as a chordophone is the lyre, or lyra. These instruments have gut strings (made from sheep intestine) that stretch between a frame, or crossbar, and a soundboard. The crossbar is supported by two arms that are attached to each side of the instrument's body. The strings are attached to the soundboard at the string holder. Ashenafi Kebede defines the lyre on "A History Of Music" website.

An ancient Greek vase depicts Orpheus playing the lyre.

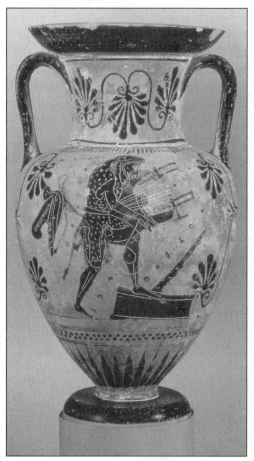

Lyres are structurally distinguished from other chordophones in the following ways: Two wooden side-posts emerge from a sound resonator; a crossbar or yoke connects the posts on the opposite side of the resonator; the strings, stretched from the crossbar down to the bottom of the resonator, always run parallel to the face of the resonator. . . . Lyres are found in many of the . . . African, Near Eastern, and Mediterranean cultures. For example, it is known as kinnor in Hebrew, kinnara in Arabic, [and] ginera in Egypt.[52]

The lyre was well known in ancient Greece and was said to be the chief instrument played by Orpheus, the child of the sun god Apollo. At that time lyres were divided by their number of strings. Some lyres were depicted with seven or fewer strings, while others held eight or more. Those with eight or more strings were played by musicians who used both hands to pluck each string separately. Those with seven or fewer strings were played in a style called "block and strum," in which the musician strums the strings with either the back of the hand or a pick held between the thumb and fingers. Meanwhile, the right-handed player uses his or her left hand to block, or mute, certain strings so they do not sound.

The Greeks utilized two basic types of the instrument. Amateurs played the bowl lyre whose body was constructed from a tortoise shell, wooden bowl, or bull skin. The box lyre—known as the kithara and played by professionals—had hollow, symmetrical arms attached to a hollow wooden boxlike body that was square or rectangular. According to Frederic V. Grunfeld, in *The Art and Times of the Guitar,* for more than one thousand years the kithara "reigned as the chief instrument of the public games and religious festivals of Greece and Rome."[53]

The lyre was carried to the British Isles by the Roman conquerors and may be seen in ancient pictures made

The Ethiopian Lyre

On "A History of Music" website, Ashenafi Kebede discusses the lyre still played today in Africa:

Ethiopia is the only country in the world where the box-lyre begena is found as part of the living tradition today. Wood from eucalyptus or juniper trees is ordinarily used in making the frame of the soundbox. It is then covered by parchment made of ox-hide. The box is sometimes made of a hollowed-out piece of wood of appropriate circumference and depth. The begena do not have rattles on their surface as some of the other African lyres do, such as the lyres of Uganda and Zaire, for example.

The begena plays a semi-sacred role in the hands of the solo performer. Though completely out of the sphere of the strictly sacred practices of the dominant religions, it is not either used in the performance of really secular music. For example, it is primarily used to accompany Dawit's (Biblical David's) Psalms during Lent or other fasting periods of the Christian population; again, members of the Fellasha (Black Jews) use it in a similar manner. Consequently, and following oral tradition, it is nicknamed "Dawit's Harp"; it is the instrument, they say, that David played to soothe King Saul's nerves and saved him from madness. It is also claimed that the instrument was introduced to Ethiopia by the Israelites who came to Axum from Jerusalem escorting Menelik I, the alleged son of Solomon and Queen Sheba. On the other hand, the begena is found depicted on Ethiopian manuscripts of the early fifteenth century.

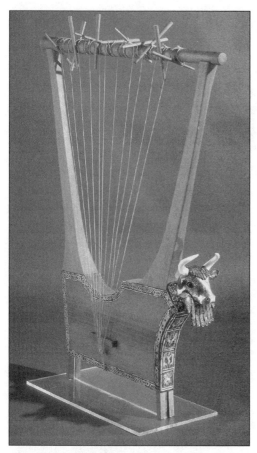

A bull's head adds a decorative element to this reconstruction of a lyre from 2500 B.C.

as long ago as the tenth century. By this time the instrument had undergone some changes, as described by Hortense Panum in *The Stringed Instruments of the Middle Ages:*

> In its soft outlines it differs decidedly from its sharply cut predecessor, for in it the arms and yoke are fused into a hoop, giving the instrument a certain resemblance to a padlock. From a narrow tail-

piece fastened to the base of the sound-box, the strings proceed to the pegs which are placed at wide intervals in the curve of the hoop. From its shape this lyre must, to differentiate it from the antique form, be characterised as the round lyre.[54]

The round lyre had seven strings and was most often played with a bow rather than plucked. Because it was difficult to play, the popularity of the lyre declined. A type of bowed lyre, however, is still played in some places, such as Finland and Estonia.

The Ancient Harp

Like the lyre, the harp is an instrument dating back to the days of ancient Babylon and Egypt. There are three basic harp shapes: the bowed or arched harp, the angle harp, and the triangle or frame harp that resembles the modern harp.

The harp is played by plucking the strings that run between a sound box and a neck. These strings run at a ninety-degree angle to the sound box instead of parallel, as on a violin.

The bow-shaped harp is the most ancient of instruments and does not resemble the modern harp because it lacks a front pillar. Instead, this instrument, depicted on paintings more than five thousand years ago, looks like a five- or six-stringed hunting bow. Musicians knelt on the ground and rested the curved part of the bow on their shoulder when playing.

Ancient Egyptians played the bow-shaped harp (left) by kneeling on the ground and resting the bow on their shoulders.

Sound boxes, or even drums, were eventually added to the bottom part of the harp to amplify the sound of the strings. Over time, these boxes were enlarged and ornately painted. The bases of Egyptian temple harps were decorated with sphinx heads, and the bow part, which extended up to six feet, was decorated with mosaic tiles.

As the harp traveled through other cultures, its shape was changed. The angle harp utilizes two posts at a right angle with strings stretched between them. These harps were played in Assyria and ancient Greece.

In the ninth century, the triangular frame harp evolved in medieval Europe and was seen in rock carvings in En-gland and Ireland. These harps differed from earlier instruments in that they were made of three solid parts, in the shape of a triangle, with strings stretched across the middle. The addition of the extra part, known as a forepillar, gave the instrument a more solid construction and greater strength. This, in turn, allowed thicker strings to be used, which gave the harp greater volume and notes that sustained, or rang, for longer periods of time.

The triangular frame harp is believed to have originated in the Scandinavian countries and was brought to northern Europe and the British Isles by Vikings. In fact the word *harp* comes from an Old Norse word that means "to pluck." This term was widely used for the frame harp by the thirteenth century.

The strings of the harp are enclosed by a frame, and the instrument is supported by a pillar outside the longest string. On the "Gaelic Harps and Harpers in Ireland and Scotland" website, Robert Ruadh describes the ancient instrument that had thirty to fifty strings and was played by musicians who plucked them with long fingernails:

> The harp played by the Irish and Scottish harpers of the old Gaelic order was an aristocratic instrument, played in the courts of kings and before the chiefs of clans. It was much like other non-pedal harps in use in our own time, but differs in that it was strung with bronze wire rather than gut or nylon. Its sound-box was carved in one piece out of wood from the bog. It had other-worldly associations, and in the hands of a master harper had power over its listeners to bring them great joy, or cause them to weep with sorrow, or lull them to sleep. . . .

> Music was an important part of life in ancient Ireland, and professional harpers were honored above all other musicians. In social position the harper ranked at the top of the *bó-aire* class of nobility, who were without land of their own, but whose wealth was in cattle. There may have been

harp schools in Ireland, as there certainly were in Wales . . . where harpers spent several years in intensive training.[55]

The Modern Harp

The pedal harp used in modern orchestras is a frame harp also known as the concert or grand harp. The average concert grand weighs about ninety pounds and is slightly more than six feet tall. These are made of maple wood and have forty-six strings, covering six-and-one-half octaves with seven strings per octave. The bass, or lower, strings are made from wound wire, while the treble, or upper, strings are made from gut or nylon. The proper harpist uses only the thumb and first three fingers of each hand to play—the little finger is never used.

In the eighteenth century, to broaden the harp's range, pedals were added to raise and lower the strings and produce "accidentals"—sharp or flat notes outside the seven-note scale. On "The Harp" website, Paul Huang explains how the complicated pedal setup works on a modern instrument:

> The harp has a system of seven double action pedals, each pedal controlling one string in every octave. Three of the pedals are controlled by the left foot and four by the right. Each pedal has three positions which are held in place by notches in the base of the harp. These positions shorten the length of the strings forming sharps or

Harpists play their instrument by plucking strings that are attached to a triangular wooden frame.

flats. For example, the harp is tuned in C flat. When the "C" pedal is in the highest of the three notches, all the "C" strings will sound as C flat. When the pedal is in the middle notch, the notes will be C natural and in the lowest notch they will be C sharp. By using these pedals, the accomplished harpist can play the chromatic scale.[56]

Although the harp produces beautiful, "heavenly" music, few composers have written parts for the instrument. It was mainly used for its swirling special effect in opera, although famous composers such as Haydn, Rossini, Frédéric Chopin, and others were harp players. Mozart only used the instrument in one piece, as did Beethoven. Perhaps the musician who did most to promote the harp in the twentieth century was, ironically, the outrageous silent comedian Harpo Marx, a member of the renowned Marx Brothers. Harpo was a talented, classically trained musician who only went into comedy to support his family. His harp performances, however, are memorable additions to the classic Marx Brothers movies.

The Lute

In addition to the harp and the lyre, a third type of chordophone, the lute, originated in ancient times. Modern instruments from the tiny ukulele to the huge stand-up bass owe their basic shape and structure to the ancient lute.

With a neck and fingerboard attached to a shell or drumlike body, primitive lutelike instruments are still made in their original ancient style in Morocco. Frederic V. Grunfeld describes the construction and importance of the fingerboard in *The Art and Times of the Guitar:*

> It is the principle of the thing that matters; the principle of the fingerboard, which seems perfectly obvious but must have represented a major technological breakthrough in its time. Both the harp and the lyre were designed basically to produce only one note per string . . . to play a variety of tones, one needed a lot of

This figurine from ancient China plays a four-stringed lute.

strings. The lute had few strings, but by pressing them against the fingerboard—*i.e.,* by "stopping" the strings—the player had access to a whole gamut of tones. Musically, in an age of melody, the lutes opened up a new range of microtonal possibilities, just as later, in medieval Europe, they were to suggest new patterns of harmony.[57]

Like the guitar in later centuries, the ancient lute seems to have been used most commonly to play "folk" songs, as opposed to martial and religious music. And echoing the hoopla surrounding rock and roll today, lute players were sometimes shown surrounded by acrobats, jugglers, snake charmers, and performing monkeys.

By the eighth century, the lute was played throughout the Arab world. The word *lute* itself is derived from the Arab *al-'ud,* meaning "wood," so named either because it had a soundboard made from wood, as opposed to animal skin, or because the body was constructed from wooden strips, rather than a gourd or tortoise shell. About twelve other instruments, both large and small, were based on the *al-'ud.*

An unnamed tenth-century author enthusiastically describes the musician performing an *al-'ud* recital:

> He played . . . [the strings] in a kind of way that made everyone in the assembly laugh from the

The Mandolin

On "A Brief History of the Mandolin" website, Dan Beimborn discusses that instrument.

The mandolin can be described as a small, short-necked lute with eight strings. A lute is a chordophone, an instrument which makes sound by the vibration of strings. As a descendent of the lute, the mandolin reaches back to some of the earliest musical instruments. . . .

In a gallery in Washington, a painting by Agnelo Gaddi (1369–1396) depicts an angel playing a miniature lute called the mandora. The miniature lute was probably contrived to fill out the scale of 16th century lute ensembles. The Assyrians called this new instrument a Pandura, which described its shape. The Arabs called it Dambura, the Latins Mandora, the Italians, Mandola. The smaller version of the traditional mandola was called mandolina by the Italians.

The mandolin entered the mainstream of popular American culture during the first epoch of substantial immigration from eastern and southern Europe, a period of prosperity and vulgarity, when things exotic and foreign dominated popular taste.

It was in vogue in the 1850s, when it shared the parlor with zithers, mandolas, ukuleles, and other novelties designed to amuse the increasingly leisured middle class. . . . The mandolin was even among the first recorded instruments on Edison cylinders. In 1897, Montgomery Ward's catalog marveled at the "phenomenal growth in our Mandolin trade." . . .

The 1905 Gibson A-4 was a revolutionary instrument in its time, breaking radically away from the traditional bowl-back instruments brought to America by Italian immigrants. . . . Instead of having a flat or bent top and a bowlback, [Gibson's] new design was based on principles of violin construction, using a carved top and back. Though this design was subtly modified over the years, it clearly set the standard for what was to become the preferred style of mandolin used in American folk and popular music.

merriment and pleasure, joy and gladness, which entered their souls. Then he altered . . . [the strings] and played them in another way, and made them all weep from the sadness of the mode . . . and grief of heart. Then he altered them again, and played them again, and made everyone go to sleep.[58]

The *al-'ud* was brought to Spain by the Moors during their occupation of that country from 711 to 1492. By the thirteenth century, the instrument had lost its connection to Arab musicians and was widespread throughout Europe.

In the sixteenth century, the lute was known as the "Queen of European Instruments."[59] German and Italian lute makers turned out thousands of instruments a year. These generally were made of sycamore or ash and had long, narrow bodies with nine or eleven broad ribs on the back. The eight to ten strings—arranged in five pairs, or courses—were attached at the rounded base by a guitarlike tailpiece. Later a sixth, single string was added. Four to nine frets were attached to the neck so musicians could accurately place their fingers on the fretboard in order to play the proper notes. These frets were made of gut tied around the neck and spaced at chromatic intervals.

Similarly to other instruments such as the oboe, lutes were made in many sizes so that they could play in different registers. The smallest was the octave lute, followed by the small treble, treble, alto, tenor, bass, and large octave lute.

Books and sheet music from the sixteenth century show that the lute was used to play dances, short introductory pieces of music called preludes, and polyphonic songs. Panum explains:

[Lutenists] adapted to their instrument all the music performed in church and in public, thus giving the lovers of the lute an opportunity of benefiting by it at home. Moreover, these lute-books were by no means content with merely giving the public a collection of pieces; in most cases they also gave elaborate instructions for tuning and playing the lute as well as instructions in the art of writing the [music], in fingering, and in the placing of the frets, etc. The text is generally homely and intimate. The reader is always admonished to listen carefully to what is said. The lute-books were also often used to perpetuate moral advice, and even questions of [religious] doctrine.[60]

The lute remained a fashionable instrument for the middle and upper classes throughout the eighteenth century. Bach, Haydn, and Mozart added to the already voluminous reams of compositions for the lute. By the end of the eighteenth century, however, the instrument was eclipsed by the violin, guitar, and mandolin. With little fanfare, the instrument that provided the basis for dozens of stringed instruments faded from public view.

The Violin and Viola

The lute was a limited instrument in many ways—it was difficult to hear in crowds and, with upwards of two dozen strings in later years, a nightmare to keep in tune. The four-string violin, on the other hand, was loud, capable of expressing a wide range of musical emotion, easy to carry, and versatile enough to play the most complicated of classical music pieces.

The modern violin has changed little since the Middle Ages. It has the highest pitch of any stringed instrument, except the ukulele, and the four strings are tuned in musical fifths—that is, G, D, A, and E. The strings are attached to four tuning pegs pressed into what is known as a pegbox. And ever since the eighteenth century, the pegbox has been traditionally topped with a carved scroll. An arched back provides the instrument with a greater depth of sound, and two f-holes in the soundboard give the violin its volume.

The strings of the violin are played with a bow, a flexible stick about thirty inches long, strung with horsehair. Bows are most likely based on hunting bows, and were first used to play primitive instruments more than ten thousand years ago.

While playing the violin, the right-handed musician places the left hand on the fretless neck and presses the

The modern violin is a versatile instrument that is represented in almost all genres of music.

The Stradivari violin is an expertly crafted eighteenth-century instrument esteemed by serious musicians and collectors.

strings down on the fingerboard. The right hand and arm is used to draw the bow back and forth at a right angle across the strings.

The first bowed instruments were depicted in European illustrations around the tenth century A.D., but the modern violin is a combination of several instruments popular over the next five centuries.

It is believed that the first violin was originally adapted from the Moorish rebec, an instrument that itself was based on the lute. This pear-shaped instrument was carved and hollowed out from a single block of wood. Around the twelfth century, the medieval fiddle

appeared, and this was constructed from flat pieces of wood formed into a spade shape. Around 1490 the viol appeared in Italy and Spain. This was a largish six-string violin-like instrument with frets, and it was played while resting in an upright position on the musician's lap. Italy was also home to the *lire da braccio,* a seven-stringed instrument that was held under the neck and played with a bow, much like the modern violin.

The names used for the instrument help show its evolution. The original term comes from *fides,* the Roman word for "strings." This term evolved into *fidicula,* used to define the kithara, and

The Cello

On the "Instrumentally Speaking . . . The Cello" website, Paul Huang describes the instrument:

The cello, also called the violoncello is a large, low-pitched musical instrument of the violin family, the true bass of the violin. However, in build it differs somewhat, the ribs being proportionately much deeper and the much higher bridge standing on legs rather than feet. It is about 27½ inches long (47 inches with the neck). The neck is raked back at a sharper angle to allow for the height of the bridge. The cello is held between the knees while it rests on an end pin, which is telescoped through the tailpin and can be clamped in any position to adjust the height of the instrument above the floor. It has four strings, pitched C-G-D-A upward from two octaves below middle C and has a very wide range of four octaves.

The cello has always been a vital part of the orchestra, filling out the bass-lines above the double-basses and the mainstay of the string quartet or piano trio. It is currently enjoying something of a boom, in repertoire, recording, and playing, with plenty of excellent players around. This is probably due to the similarity of the cello to the human shape and voice. As composer Jonathan Harvey puts it, "The cello is very anthropomorphic. It has the size and shape of a human being, more than any other instrument, and matches the male and female voice range almost exactly."

The cello is a large, bowed string instrument of the violin family.

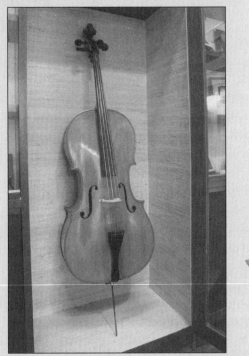

as Grunfeld writes: "In due course fides-fidicula became fidula or vitula in medieval Latin, vielle in French, viula in Provençal, videle or fiedel in German, fithele or fiddle in English, viola and violino in Italian, vihuela in Spanish."[61]

By the time of the Renaissance, the violin and viol were the prime instruments of Italy and the city of Cremona was known as the Town of Violins because so many world-class violin makers worked there. As Anna Alice Chapin writes in *The Heart of Music: The Story of the Violin:*

> [The] full-toned, delicate, perfectly balanced violins of Cremona were made to fit the surging demand for instruments more sensitive and responsive, more warmly flexible in tone, and better adapted to a long, varying gamut of musical expressions.[62]

By the 1600s violins were being used more often in orchestras. Claudio Monteverde, a Cremona native who learned to play the viol at age sixteen, transformed music forever by writing, among his other groundbreaking work, the first true opera, *Orfeo,* in 1607. In the early 1700s, renowned Cremona violin maker Antonio Stradivari made subtle changes in the varnish and structure of his violins to give them a brighter, richer tone.

By the late seventeenth century, violins and related instruments were favored by composers, orchestras, and conductors. In 1689, one orchestra in Rome reportedly had forty violins, ten violas, seventeen cellos, and seven double basses. (The cello is a large, low-pitched member of the violin family that sounds in the range beneath the violin but above the four-string upright bass, double bass, or contrabass, which is the lowest-pitched member of the violin family. Standing over six feet tall, the bass is also the largest member of the violin family.) This orchestra also contained several trumpets, a trombone, and a lute. Conversely, average church trios utilized only two violins and a bass.

The eighteenth century gave rise to the string quartet, which featured two violins, a cello, and a viola, which was tuned an octave above the cello. Composers such as Bach, Haydn, and Mozart all wrote well-known pieces for quartets.

By the nineteenth century, the violin was one of the most common instruments in the world, and its popularity had driven the viol out of fashion. Orchestras were often half composed of violin players, and the instrument was played by rich and poor alike. European Gypsies utilized the instrument for rousing folk music, and American pioneers played violins at Saturday night dances to accompany jigs, reels, waltzes, and quadrilles.

In the twentieth century, besides its traditional place in the orchestra, the violin has been played in ragtime, jazz, blues, bluegrass, country, and rock and roll. As one of the most versatile stringed instruments, the violin has found a place in almost every form of music.

The Guitar

Like the violin, the bodies of ancient lutes often had hourglass shapes that resembled guitars, but it was not until 1265 that the instrument was specifically mentioned in books or poems. By the sixteenth century, the guitar was a staple of Spanish music and commonly found throughout Europe.

The guitar is a plucked chordophone with a neck. It is about three feet long and often has a flat back, an hourglass shape, and a flat piece called a headstock at the end of the neck, to which tuning pegs are attached. Modern guitars have six strings. On Spanish, or classical, guitars the strings are made from gut or nylon, with the thickest strings made from silk spun over metal. On other acoustic and electric guitars, the strings are made from steel, nickel-plated steel, and bronze. They are tuned—from lowest to highest—to the notes E, A, D, G, B, and E.

The strings are stretched over a fingerboard that has metal frets. Atop the neck is the tuning head. Classical and acoustic guitars are generally made with a spruce top, or soundboard, and a hardwood back. When the strings are strummed or plucked, the sound emanates from a round hole in the soundboard. Right-handed players use their hand to produce sound with their fingers, fingernails, or picks while the left hand stops the strings behind the frets to make notes and chords.

The guitarist has the ability to play loud, ringing chords, single-note lead patterns, or plucked melodies utilizing several strings at a time. Throughout the centuries, this feature has made the instrument extremely popular. For example, an average of 1.5 million guitars are sold every year, compared with around 375,000 woodwinds and 142,000 pianos.

The guitar is also extremely versatile. According to Tony Bacon in *The Ultimate Guitar Book:*

> The guitar is a unique musical instrument; no other combines in such a portable package such inherent harmonic, melodic and rhythmic potential. Even played on its own, the guitar offers a remarkable range of harmony to the player, who has continuous access to over three octaves (four on many modern electrics), with polyphony limited only by the guitarist's dexterity and the musical context.[63]

Pleasant to Hear, Easy to Learn

The guitar evolved from the lute by the 1300s after it was imported to Spain by the Moors. At that time, there were two types of guitars: the almond-shaped *guiterre morische,* or Moorish guitar, and the hourglass-shaped *guitterre latine,* or Latin guitar. The *guitterre latine* had three pairs, or courses, of similarly tuned strings, plus a single high string. These were tuned, from lowest to highest: C, F, A, and D.

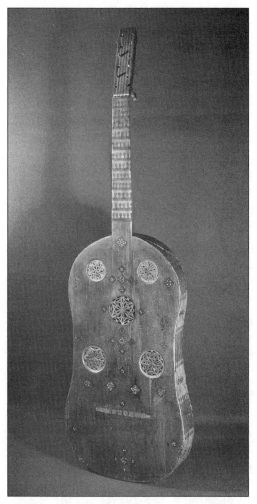

This guitar was probably created in Spain around 1500.

player—Luis de Briçeño explained why the instrument was so fashionable:

> The guitar is . . . convenient and appropriate to singing, playing, ballet-dancing, jumping, running, folk-dancing and shoedancing. I can serenade with it, singing and expressing with its help a thousand amorous passions. . . . In my and many other people's opinion, the guitar has a great advantage over the lute, which requires many attentions to be properly maintained: it has to be a good instrument, well played, well strung, and listened to carefully, in silence. But the guitar . . . whether well played or badly played, well strung or badly strung, is pleasant to hear and listen to; being so easy to learn, it attracts the busiest of talented people and makes them put aside loftier occupations so that they may hold a guitar in their hands. They desert the lute, mandora, harp, violin, sinfonia, lyre, theorbo, cittern, and clavichord, all for the guitar. Many things could be said in favor of these instruments, but here one consideration is paramount: two thousand people now entertain themselves and express their thoughts and troubles through the guitar.[64]

By the 1600s the first books of guitar notation, known as tablature, were published for the four-course, or eight-string, guitar in Spain. These instruction books helped boost the popularity of the guitar, which between the sixteenth and nineteenth centuries began to challenge the status of the lute, particularly in Spain, Italy, and France. In 1626, author—and guitar

As more people learned to play the guitar—including French king Louis

XIV and English king Charles II—the instrument underwent many changes. A fifth course was added around 1600 and a sixth by the end of the 1700s. Around 1800 these double-string courses were replaced by single strings, and the modern tuning became standard.

During the last half of the nineteenth century, guitar maker Antonio de Torres Jurado produced a lighter guitar

The Banjo

On the "Thumbnail History of the Banjo" website, Bill Reese describes the history of the ancient African instrument that was once played by slaves but is now used primarily for bluegrass music:

Banjos belong to a family of instruments that is very old. Drums with strings stretched over them can be traced throughout the Far East, the Middle East and Africa, almost from the beginning. . . . The banjo, as we can begin to recognize it, was made by African slaves, based on instruments that were indigenous to their parts of Africa. These early "banjos" were spread to the colonies of those countries engaged in the slave trade. Scholars have found that many of these instruments have names that are related to the modern word "banjo," such as "banjar," "banjil," "banza," "bangoe," "bangie," "banshaw." . . .

White men began using blackface as a comic gimmick before the American Revolution. The banjo became a prop for these entertainers, either individually or in groups. . . .

From the 1840s through the 1890s the minstrel show was not the only place to see banjo players. There are records of urban banjo contests and tournaments held at hotels, race tracks and bars, especially in New York, to the enthusiastic cheering and clapping of sometimes inebriated crowds. . . .

During most of this time, the banjo was looked-down upon by the more well-to-do classes of the population. Articles in the papers of the day, like that in the *Boston Daily Evening Voice* of 1866, classified the banjo of the 1840s and 1850s as an instrument in "the depth of popular degradation," an instrument fit only for "the jig-dancing lower classes of the community. . . . " By 1866, however, the instrument had become a "universal favorite," with over 10,000 instruments in use in Boston alone.

with a more resonant sound that resembled today's modern instrument. He also got rid of the troublesome tied-on gut frets and replaced them with metal or ivory.

Meanwhile the guitar had moved to American shores and was a favorite instrument, along with the banjo, of African Americans in the rural South. Being poor, many black musicians made their own guitars from boxes and lumber. For instance, blues legend Muddy Waters said, "All the kids make they own git-tars. Made mine out of a box and a bit of stick for a neck. Couldn't do much with it, but you know, that's how you learn."[65]

The guitar also followed pioneers west across the plains, and was popular among cowboys and rural folk. Eventually, guitarists playing black blues music mixed it up with white country twang, or "hillbilly" music, and rock and roll was born.

The Electric Guitar

In the twentieth century, sophisticated musicians such as Django Reinhardt and Charlie Christian were able to wring incredible jazz music from the guitar. In the 1930s, Christian became one of the first guitarists to solo on the electric guitar. As the instrument gained popularity, the Rickenbacker Company began to manufacture electric guitars commercially. The first Rickenbacker electric was called the "Frying Pan" because the small, round, aluminum body resembled a cooking implement.

Electric guitars rely on an electromagnetic device known as a pickup, which acts as a microphone to transmit the vibration of the strings through a wire cord to an amplifier. The tone and volume of the pickup are controlled on the guitar by knobs that may be adjusted. While the first electric guitars had only one pickup, modern guitars may have up to five, with two or three being standard. Pickups come in a variety of wiring configurations, some geared for lead guitar sounds, others for rhythm or bass tones.

After the initial development, companies such as Gibson began making

The Fender Stratocaster features a vibrato bar that allows a rapid pitch change.

the "Electric Spanish" guitar in the mid-1930s. This guitar resembled a standard instrument, except that it had f-holes and a pickup attached near the bridge. In the 1950s, California native Leo Fender began producing the first commercially available "solid body" electric guitar. The Fender Broadcaster was solid wood with a bolt-on neck made for mass production. The guitar was solid ash and had a three-way switch to allow the player to choose combinations between the treble pickup and the bass pickup.

The Broadcaster was soon renamed the Telecaster and remains in production today, along with the wildly popular three-pickup Fender Stratocaster, first produced in 1954. The "Strat" features a vibrato, or "whammy," bar built into the bridge, which allows players to rapidly change the pitch of the strings. While Fender cemented his place in history with his six-string electric guitars, he also invented the four-string bass guitar, now a staple of every band from rock to jazz to blues.

With the advent of rock and roll in the mid-1950s, hundreds of thousands of young people picked up guitars. Guitar sales in 1950 were about 228,000. By 1959 that number had jumped to 400,000. In 1963 alone, the number of guitars sold doubled from the year before—from 300,000 to 600,000. By 1965, that number had soared to 1.5 million, and Fender alone was selling 1,500 guitars a week.

By the late 1960s, Jimi Hendrix was producing music from his Strat that was as unearthly as it was unique. Using his infinite range of sounds, including long sustain, "fuzz," wah-wah, and other effects, Hendrix proved that the electric guitar could transcend almost any musical boundaries.

From the relaxing sounds of a quietly plucked lute in ancient Greece to the screaming crescendo of the electric guitar, stringed instruments have changed the sounds of music for thousands of years. Whether played in love songs of the Italian Renaissance or modern-day rock music, the sounds made by lutes, violins, cellos, banjos, mandolins, guitars, and other chordophones have greatly enriched life throughout the centuries.

Chapter Five

Keyboards

Wind, percussion, and stringed instruments have been popular throughout the centuries because they are relatively simple to make and easy to carry. On the other hand, keyboards such as organs, harpsichords, and pianos are late arrivals to the family of instruments, since they are complicated to play, expensive to make, and sometimes nearly impossible to move. The modern piano, for example, weighs hundreds of pounds and has nearly 10,000 separate parts, compared with 150 parts in a valve trumpet and about half that many in an acoustic guitar.

Keyboards are defined as musical instruments in which sound is produced by a vibrator that is activated mechanically or electronically by a person striking keys, levers, or foot pedals. The vibrator may be strings in a piano and harpsichord, or pipes in an organ. The movement of the fingers, hands, and feet supply the mechanical force to strike or pluck the strings, or activate air to vibrate pipes in an organ.

The Ancient Organ

Like many other modern instruments, the first keyboards were made from a combination of several primitive music makers joined together. For example, the early organ consisted of a wind instrument—the trumpet—joined with a forced-air concept seen on bagpipes. Those two inventions were joined on the ancient organ, known as the *hydraulos* (literally "water flute"), invented in Alexandria, Egypt, around 246 B.C. by a single inventor named Ctesibius. His instrument used a wind pump—actually a vase with a close-fitting movable valve inside that could be filled with water. The valve forced air through a hole in the bottom of the vase into several differently pitched flutes or trumpets. Metal sliders under each horn were pushed in by the finger, thus allowing air into specific pipes.

A woman plays an organ (right) in this second-century Roman statuette.

Each produced a loud musical note. The mechanical sliders had springs that closed them when not in use. Later the sliders were attached to a keyboard mechanism—that is, a set of levers or keys laid out in a row that could be struck by the fingers.

The water vase was eventually replaced in Roman times by several men who blew into a large wooden box known as an air-storage chest. This stored air could be let out under controlled conditions to play pipes fitted with reeds. Later pleated leather bags that could be pumped up and down to produce air, called bellows, were operated by Roman slaves. In *The Story of the Organ,* C.F. Abdy Williams describes how this instrument was used:

The instrument which began in this humble manner not only became exceedingly popular, but was for centuries a source of admiration and astonishment to the unlearned. The powerful sound, the rapidity of execution, the mysterious bubbling of the water, the exertions of the slaves, who were obliged to pump with all their might to supply the air in sufficient quantity, all combined to attract attention to it. It was used for contests in the public games; it formed part of the entertainment at feasts; it found its way into private houses; and in one instance, at least, took the place of the trumpet in giving the signal for the commencement of the brutal . . . sea-fights, which were the delight of the . . . populace.[66]

The name of the instrument itself is of Greek origin. The term *organon* was used to describe, not musical instruments, but instruments that were tools with which work, or *ergon,* was performed. As Peter Williams writes in *A New History of the Organ,* St. Augustine explained the term in 1398 while defining the instrument itself: "[*Organon*] is a generall name of all Instrumentes of Musyk: and is . . . specyally apropryte to the Instrument that is made of many pypes: and blowe[n] with belowes."[67]

Whatever the origins of the term, by the tenth century A.D., organs were found in churches throughout Europe. The Benedictine monk Theophilus describes a German instrument in the 1100s that had eight copper pipes, an air-storage, or wind chest, a wind collector, and lettered wooden sliders for each pipe that allowed the player to know which notes he was hitting.

The "King of Instruments"

By the Middle Ages, the organ had grown into one of the most complex machines ever invented until that time. Wind chests were able to house

Wind Chests

Wind chests or soundboards are the heart of the organ, containing the pipes and regulating the air. Their somewhat complicated function is described by Bernard Sonnaillon in King of Instruments:

The wind-chests look like wooden boxes on which are planted pipes of every height and every diameter. These chests contain a large number of elements vital to the functioning of the organ, since they distribute the air under pressure among the different pipes by means of a system of selection controlled by the organist.

We shall begin by describing a wind-chest of classical format, known as a blockchest. The wind, channeled from the main bellows along a large wind-trunk, is stored in a box the same length as the wind-chest. This is the pallet box. This chamber, which is hermetically sealed although it can be opened in case of need, was for a long time described as "the organ's secret," since it is the pallet box on which devolves the task of distributing the wind to the correct pipes. This lower chamber is connected to the end of the keyboard mechanisms entering through the bottom of the chest into which holes have been drilled for that purpose. Since these holes could allow air to escape through them, they are fitted with small leather membranes or diaphragms, or else with felt buttons, which ensure that the chest remains airtight. The ends of the keyboard mechanism are in turn attached to wooden valves or pallets, rectangular in shape and covered with leather. They are kept closed in a position of rest and held against the ceiling of the pallet box by means of a spring. When the organist, seated at the console, depresses a key, the movement is transmitted to the pallet, which opens to admit air to a groove.

The organ, depicted here on a fifteenth-century tapestry, was one of the most complex machines invented at that time.

dozens of pipes, and since a method was needed to play the multiple pipes, extra keyboards were added, with some organs featuring two or three keyboards along with a set of foot pedals. The development of sliders that moved under more than one pipe meant that one key could play multiple pipes, giving the organ the ability to play a single note with several different pipes for various octaves.

By 1450, some German church organs had from six to twenty-six pipes

per note. Mechanisms called stops (push-pull knobs set near the keyboard) allowed players to shut off specific pipes or add them to the chorus of notes. Unique tone colors and sound effects were made by the addition of reeds, square wooden pipes, and other inventions that were controlled by the stops. Bernard Sonnaillon describes the sound provided by some nineteenth-century pipes in *King of Instruments:*

[Some pipes] seek to imitate various sounds such as birdcalls, animal cries and the sounds of nature and of warfare: the Rossignol or Nachtigall [stops], whose tiny pipes are suspended in water so that bubbles produced by the flow of air imitate the warbling of nightingales; a barking dog, a growling bear or a braying ass produced by untuned pipes; a storm created by a mechanism (a length of wood) which holds down the lowest notes of the pedals simultaneously; the sound of beating rain suggested by means of small pebbles rolling around inside a metal drum; military percussion (Banda militare) incorporating the big drum and cymbals, or the rolling of kettledrums (Timpani) produced by means of two untuned pipes, and, finally, the Chapeau chinois in which small spherical bells are shaken against a rod, and the Zimbelstern which consists of a revolving metal star with a set of bells attached to it.[68]

Despite these later additions, the organ of 1450 differed little from the pipe organs in use today, as Nicholas Thistlewaite writes in *The Cambridge Companion to the Organ:* "It is a remarkable tribute to the medieval enterprise and craftsmanship that no significant innovations in the basic design of the organ were made for the next three centuries."[69]

As the organ grew in complexity, it also expanded in size. By the second half of the eighteenth century, several Euro-

pean churches contained spectacular organs that drew worshipers from near and far. Organ builders—some of the most respected craftsmen of their time—traveled from town to town constructing huge, expensive organs as churches competed to outdo one another.

During the early years of the eighteenth century, Johann Sebastian Bach was one of Germany's most renowned organists. In addition to writing music for the instrument, Bach also built and repaired organs, and his mastery of the instrument is legendary. After watching him test a restored organ in Cassel, Germany, rector Constantin Bellermann described Bach's incredible footwork:

Composer J.S. Bach was also a virtuoso organist.

The Accordion

The accordion is technically an aerophone because it makes music as air is forced over reeds. Despite this classification, the accordion with its buttons or keyboard has many similarities to the organ, as Henry Doktorski writes on the "Birth of the Accordion" website:

The accordion is relatively young compared to most orchestral instruments. Christoph Wagner, the author of *Das Akkordeon: Eine Wilde Karriere,* wrote, "Its date of birth is known exactly and there is even a birth certificate. It was written as a patent on the 23rd of May, 1829 for piano and organ maker Cyrill Demian [(1772–1847)] in Vienna on the invention of a new instrument, called accordion."

Demian's accordion was very simple: two key-activated diatonic [eight-tone] single-action harmonicas connected by bellows; the left side of the instrument had a few buttons which produced different chords, hence the name accordion. (Both the French word *accord* and the German word *akkord* mean chord in English.) Yet Demian's invention, however important, was simply one stage in the development of the long line of the free-reed instruments.

The evolution of the accordion began in China, sometime during the third millennium B.C., with the sheng—literally "sublime voice"—which is the earliest known example of a free-reed instrument. According to oral tradition it was invented by the female sovereign Nyn-Kwa in 3000 B.C. The sheng had a gourd as a wind-chamber and thirteen to twenty-four bamboo pipes. At the base of each pipe a tongue was cut in such a way as to vibrate freely when the player blew into the instrument through the mouthpiece and covered the hole in the side of a pipe with a finger. The sheng was formed to imitate the shape of the Phoenix bird and it is probably because of this tradition that it is still used today in China for funeral processions.

[Bach] can by the use of his feet alone (while his fingers do either nothing or something else) achieve such an admirable, agitated, and rapid concord of sounds on the church organ that others would seem unable to imitate it even with their fingers. When he was called . . . to Cassel to pronounce an organ properly restored, he ran over the pedals with this same facility, as if his feet had wings, making the organ resound with such fullness, and so penetrate the ears of those present like a thunderbolt, that . . . [the] Prince of Cassel admired him with such astonishment that he drew a ring with a precious stone from his finger and gave it to Bach as soon as the sound had died away. If Bach earned such a gift for the agility of his feet, what, I ask, would the Prince have given him if he had called his hands into service as well.[70]

Bach also wrote more than 260 compositions for the organ in his lifetime. Although he never traveled more than one hundred miles from his home in central Germany, the composer synthesized the German organ styles with those from France and Italy, changing organ music forever.

Partially in response to the complexity of Bach's music, as well as that of other composers, the organ continued to undergo changes in tone and structure. In the nineteenth century, pipes that imitated orchestral instruments were developed. These instruments inspired composers such as Franz Liszt and Max Reger to write new orchestral music for the organ.

In 1935, an entirely different sort of organ was invented in America by Laurens Hammond, who utilized electronic circuitry, vacuum tubes, and amplifiers to produce tones similar to a pipe organ. Although not really a true organ since it does not vibrate air within a pipe, the Hammond became instantly popular with traveling musicians and dance bands. And for the first time, amateur musicians could buy compact organs to play at home. By the 1960s and 1970s, the electric organ was a fixture in rock-and-roll bands such as Procol Harum and Yes, who used the Hammond to achieve a "classical" rock sound.

Zithers and Dulcimers

Before the Hammond was invented, only churches and the castles of the rich and powerful could accommodate the pipes, sound chests, and numerous keyboards found on the pipe organ. Beginning around the seventeenth century, however, musicians could obtain smaller keyboard instruments that could easily fit into the corner of a room. And like the organ, the harpsichord—forerunner to the piano—was based on an ancient instrument, in this case the zither.

The most primitive zithers were simply made from gut strings attached to bars and stretched over holes in the ground—the hole being necessary to resonate the sound of the strings. The "ground zither" evolved into board zithers and more complex instruments made from bone, stone, or reed tubes. Hollow gourds were attached to act as resonators. Like later zithers, these instruments had strings stretched between two bridges, and the strings were plucked or struck with sticks or other hammers.

By 1100 B.C., long, slim, fretted zithers with silk strings were played in China. A similar instrument, the six-foot-long koto, is still played in Japan. A ten-string, zitherlike instrument was known as the psaltery in Turkey in the 1100s (A.D.), and by the fourteenth century, the instrument had grown to encompass sixty-six strings arranged in groups of three. The dulcimer (in Latin *dulce melos,* or "sweet song") was similar to the psaltery but had strings that were meant to be played with two small padded hammers, much as piano hammers strike strings. By the seventeenth century, dulcimers were very popular among troubadours and minstrels. One of the most talented players was Pantaleon Hebenstreit of Eisleben, Germany. As David Crombie writes in *Piano:*

> [Hebenstreit] became a famous dulcimer player, wielding the instrument's hammers with a degree of showmanship that made [him] a celebrity across Europe. . . . A good dulcimer player would . . . have had considerable control over both the volume and tone of

In 1935 Laurens Hammond invented an entirely new kind of organ called the Hammond.

each individual note played, and could introduce their own expression into any piece of music. That is exactly what made Hebenstreit famous.

Such was Hebenstreit's fame as a dulcimer virtuoso that he set about redesigning the instrument to suit his talents. He greatly enlarged the instrument so that it was more than nine feet long, four times the usual size. He increased its range by providing 180 strings, and added an extra soundboard. In order to give himself a yet wider tonal spectrum he developed double-faced hammers, where each face was covered with different materials so that he could choose between a hard and a soft impact upon the strings. . . . The instrument incorporated a dynamic range unusual at the time, but the skills required to play it meant that few could master it, and its complexity and size meant that still fewer were attracted to own one. . . . But its influence was considerable . . . and is an important link between the world of keyed and non-keyed stringed instruments.[71]

The Clavichord

While Hebenstreit relied on hand power to wield musical hammers, other inventors were toying with ways to make strings resonate by more mechanical means. These innovations were seen in both the clavichord and the harpsichord, which were developed from the psaltery in the 1500s.

The clavichord's Latin name explains its function—*clavis,* or key, and *chorde,* or string. The clavichord has a rectangular case with a keyboard on the left and the soundboard on the right. Thin metal strings running parallel to the ground are attached on the right to tuning pins that can be turned to raise or lower the pitch. The strings run over a bridge set in the soundboard and are fixed solidly to the instrument by devices known as hitchpins set on the left side of the case. Early clavichords had twenty notes, with more added in the fifteenth century. By the sixteenth century, the instrument encompassed two-and-one-half octaves, and by the seventeenth that number had grown to four octaves.

When the clavichord key is depressed, a small brass blade called a tangent rises up and strikes a string, making it vibrate and produce sound. When the key is released, the string is immediately silenced by a piece of felt woven through the strings near the hitchpins. Players can produce vibrato, or fluctuations in pitch, by varying the pressure on the keys.

The felt, combined with the instrument's small soundboard, gives the clavichord a very quiet sound, which made it popular in monasteries and nunneries, where the soft music would not disturb others. Because of its small size and low cost, the instrument was also used for teaching

The clavichord, seen in this 1648 painting, produces a quiet sound, which made it popular in monasteries and nunneries.

and was fashionable at intimate gatherings in the homes of average citizens.

Harpsichords

Unlike the clavichord, the harpsichord produced a louder tone because its strings were plucked by a plectrum, or pick, made from a quill or cowhide. Musicians and composers who desired instruments for concert and ensemble use preferred the harpsichord, which was widely used from the 1700s to the early 1800s.

The clear, crisp, and clean sounds of the harpsichord's plucked metal strings made it perfect for the complex sounds of contrapuntal music—that is, music written by composers such as Bach in which two or more melodies were played simultaneously. The volume of the harpsichord arose from its long, narrow wing shape that supported a large soundboard and long, thick strings. Each string in a harpsichord has a small plectrum set in a small piece of wood called a jack, which is attached to a key. When the key is depressed, the far end raises the jack and the plectrum plucks the string. When the finger is removed from the key, the plectrum slides down without hitting the string again. With this system, the sound and tone of the instrument remains constant regardless of how much pressure is applied to the key by the musician.

String courses, or sets, of two or three were added later, and this increased the volume of the instrument. By the 1700s, some harpsichord manufacturers were adding up to five strings per note, and a second, or even third, keyboard was added. This allowed players to strike notes in a normal range with one keyboard and strike strings an octave higher with another.

The Early Piano

By the end of the 1600s, the keyboard had come a long way from the zither and the hydraulos. European citizens were familiar with huge pipe organs, clavichords, harpsichords, and other similar instruments. All of these, however, presented problems for the musician and composer, as Crombie writes:

Musicians and composers during the eighteenth and nineteenth centuries preferred the harpsichord for concert and ensemble use because of the instrument's loud, clear sounds.

None of these gave the player a satisfactory way of controlling dynamics. In other words, it was impossible to control individually the volume of each note played. This made it difficult to introduce expression to the music.

There were various ineffective solutions. The organist could change stops to give the instrument a more powerful sound. The harpsichord player could introduce extra sets of strings to make the instrument louder. The clavichord player was able to take some advantage of the instrument's limited degree of dynamic response, but it was such a quiet instrument anyway that playing more softly wasn't of practical use. The only effective way that composers could draw expression from these instruments was by actually writing in more notes when emphasis was required.[72]

The single man credited with solving all of these problems on various instruments was harpsichord maker Bartolomeo Cristofori, father of the pianoforte. Cristofori worked for Prince Ferdinand dé Medici in Florence, Italy. Although there are no records of his first piano, the world's oldest surviving piano, housed in the Metropolitan Museum of Art in New York City, was built by Cristofori in 1720. Historians believe that he constructed the first piano around 1710.

Because Cristofori's piano had the ability to resonate with so much more dynamic range than other stringed keyboards at the time, his invention was known as the pianoforte, *piano* meaning "soft" in Italian, and *forte* "loud." As Crombie writes: "The combination of the two words emphasizes the piano's potential to produce loud or soft tones depending on how hard its keys are struck."[73]

Cristofori's piano had a four-octave range with courses of strings tuned together. Like modern pianos, when the keys were depressed they activated hammers, which hit the strings. The instrument had some problems, however. For example, sometimes an individual hammer bounced back and hit a string several times when the key was hit only once. Also, the pounding of the hammer tended to break the strings until thicker strings were developed later in the century.

While the new instrument was clearly innovative, few musicians were skillful enough to play it. Organ and harpsichord players had a difficult time regulating how hard they depressed the keys, and no pianofortes existed outside of Florence, Italy. Cristofori built only about twenty of the instruments before he died at the age of seventy-five in 1731.

The English Viennese Schools

By 1760, pianofortes were not being made in Italy, but instead were being manufactured mainly in Germany, Austria, and England. In fact, some of the best pianos were made by German craftsmen for the Broadwood Company based in London, England. Small models, known as the "English Square," cost less than half the price of a standard harpsichord. A member of the Broadwood family described the look and sound of the instrument:

> They were in length about four feet, the hammers very lightly covered with a thin coat of leather; the strings were small, nearly the size of those used on the Harpsichord; the tones clear, what is now called thin and wiry—[the] object being, seemingly, to approach the tones of the Harpsichord, to which the ear, at that period, was accustomed.[74]

By the 1770s, the piano was taking on unique and inventive shapes and sizes. Lightweight boxes with keys, soundboard, strings—and sometimes no legs—were called portable pianos and were enjoyed by students and traveling musicians. An instrument known as the "sewing box" was a real piano with two-and-one-half octaves. With its 9½-by-13½-inch case about six inches tall, it could be set on any table. An instrument known as an *orphica* had a keyboard and hammers attached to a small harplike instrument, which could be worn around the neck with a leather strap.

While novelty pianos were popular with the public, the highest-quality instruments were the Viennese pianos, re-sembling baby grands, built by Johann Andreas Stein. In 1830, composer Friedrich Kalkbrenner described the difference between pianos made in the Viennese style and those made in London:

> The instruments of Vienna and London have produced two different schools. The pianists of Vienna are especially distinguished for the precision, clearness and rapidity of their execution; the instruments fabricated in that city are extremely easy to play, and, in order to avoid confusion of sound, they are made with mufflers [dampers] up to the last high note; from this results a great dryness in [sustained] passages, as one sound does not flow into another. In Germany the use of the pedals is scarcely known. English pianos possess rounder sounds and a somewhat heavier touch; they have caused the professors of that country to adopt a grander style, and that beautiful manner of singing which distinguishes them; to succeed in this, the use of the loud pedal is indispensable, in order to conceal the dryness inherent to the pianoforte.[75]

Perhaps the most eminent player of the Viennese school was Mozart, who learned to play the harpsichord when he was three years old and probably encountered his first piano at the age of about eighteen. While the composer wrote most of his early sonatas and concertos for the harpsichord, others

Young Mozart (seated) became a talented piano player and composer and helped popularize the instrument among the nobility.

transforming the way the piano was played, as Crombie writes:

> Liszt was a revolutionary in romantic music and was recognised as the greatest pianist of his day. His playing style both excited and delighted audiences. He became totally engrossed in his playing, and as a result his emotions took control. Coupled with his remarkably strong hands, this resulted in the destruction of many a piano, especially at the beginning of his career when instruments were less robust.[77]

may have been written with the piano in mind. Whatever the case, the renowned composer was a talented pianist, as David Rowland writes in *The Cambridge Companion to the Piano:* "One of the most noteworthy aspects of Mozart's expressive performance was his use of *rubato;* not the constant changing of tempo which is adopted by many pianists today, but a technique whereby the two hands do not quite synchronise."[76]

With composers such as Mozart leading the way, the piano continued to grow in popularity, especially among the nobility and royalty. In the 1790s the grand piano was developed with six octaves—one more than the standard of the day. By the mid-nineteenth century, composers such as Franz Liszt were

Pianos for the People

Throughout the nineteenth century, instrument makers continued to improve and change the piano. Octaves were added until the piano had eighty-eight keys, and heavier hammers, thicker strings, and iron frames were made to improve durability, loudness, and tone. Away from the concert hall, the piano was seen as an instrument of refinement that even average workers could strive to own. To fill this lucrative market, piano makers began to build smaller, less expensive models for the home.

By the end of the century, player pianos came into vogue. These instruments could play automatically, utilizing a long roll of paper with holes punched in it that turned levers to activate hammers on the strings. At first these were cranked by hand, later by electric motors. Taverns and amusement parks featured player pianos that

Electronic Keyboards

While electricity has been used to power instruments since the late nineteenth century, the first widely used electronic keyboard instruments did not come into vogue until the mid–twentieth century. After the electric Hammond organ was invented in 1935, it was not until the early 1960s that the first electric piano, the Wurlitzer EP200, came into use, particularly in rock bands. This instrument utilized a keyboard that activated hammers that struck flat reeds, which vibrated and were converted to electrical signals by electrostatic pickups.

The sound of the electronic keyboard was revolutionized again by Robert Moog (rhymes with "vogue"), who made one of the first commercially available synthesizers with keyboard-activated transistorized circuits capable of producing sound. These circuits used electric voltage to create and control sounds. Higher voltages made higher notes and lower voltages lower notes. Musician Walter Carlos popularized the Moog synthesizer with his mid-sixties album *Switched on Bach.*

In 1972, the Japanese company Rowland released the first inexpensive analog synthesizer that generated a wide array of sound effects. By the early 1980s, the first computerized digital synthesizers were in production. These programmable instruments could imitate pianos, organs, horns, woodwinds, or nearly any other sound imaginable. Since that time, the capabilities of musical keyboard synthesizers has paralleled that of the modern computer even as the price has fallen. Modern synthesizers have built-in drum machines and can play a nearly infinite variety of musical sounds.

Walter Carlos sits at his keyboard and synthesizer.

operated only after patrons inserted coins into a pay box.

As pianos became more available to the average citizen, music changed along with the instruments. In the early years of the 1900s, a style called ragtime was developed by African American performers in saloons and minstrel theaters.

Written specifically for the piano, ragtime is syncopated music in which the melody is played with the right hand while a "walking" bass line is played on the left. This music was extremely difficult to play—so difficult, in fact, that most of it was disseminated to the general public via player pianos that could be "programmed" to play the complex tunes. The leading proponent of ragtime was Scott Joplin, whose 1899 composition "Maple Leaf Rag" began the national ragtime craze and went on to sell over one million copies of sheet music.

After the ragtime fad had passed in 1910, other African American musicians continued to revolutionize piano music. The instrument was utilized by Jelly Roll Morton, who took 1920s jazz to new heights. In later years, blues and boogie-woogie pianists inspired rock-and-roll players such as "Little Richard" Penniman, Jerry Lee Lewis, and others.

Jazz pioneer Jelly Roll Morton helped revolutionize piano music.

While the piano has a shorter history than almost any other musical instrument, it has shaped and influenced the sound of music practically from its first incarnation in Cristofori's studio. From the startling opening chords of Beethoven's Ninth Symphony to the rollicking rock of "Good Golly Miss Molly," the hammering notes emitted by the piano's eighty-eight keys continue to inspire and delight more than four centuries after the instrument was born.

• Notes •

Introduction: The Sounds of Music

1. Keith Spence, *Living Music*. New York: Gloucester Press, 1979, p. 8.

Chapter One: Percussion

2. Mickey Hart with Jay Stevens, *Drumming at the Edge of Magic*. San Francisco: HarperCollins, 1990, p. 70.
3. Hart, *Drumming at the Edge of Magic*, p. 34.
4. Töm Klöwer, *The Joy of Drumming*. Diever, Holland: Binkey Kok Publications, 1997, p. 68.
5. Bernard S. Mason, *Drums, Tomtoms, and Rattles*. New York: Dover Publications, 1974, p. 171.
6. James Blades, *Percussion Instruments and their History*. London: Faber and Faber, 1974, pp. 37–38.
7. Charles L. White, *Drums Through the Ages*. Los Angeles: Sterling Press, 1960, p. 64.
8. Blades, *Percussion Instruments and their History*, p. 45.
9. Blades, *Percussion Instruments and their History*, p. 45.
10. Hart, *Drumming at the Edge of Magic*, p. 38.
11. Layne Redmond, *When the Drummers Were Women*. New York: Three Rivers Press, 1997, p. 19.
12. Blades, *Percussion Instruments and their History*, p. 51.
13. White, *Drums Through the Ages*, pp. 140–41.
14. White, *Drums Through the Ages*, p. 147.
15. Hart, *Drumming at the Edge of Magic*, p. 61.
16. Hart, *Drumming at the Edge of Magic*, p. 18.

Chapter Two: Woodwinds

17. Raymond Meylan, *The Flute*. Portland, OR: Amadeus Press, 1988, p. 13.
18. Meylan, *The Flute*, p. 52.
19. James Galway, *Flute*. New York: Schirmer Books, 1982, pp. 18–19.
20. Quoted in Galway, *Flute*, p. 22.
21. Quoted in Meylan, *The Flute*, p. 114.
22. Nancy Toff, *The Development of the Modern Flute*. New York: Taplinger Publishing, 1979, pp. 45–46.
23. Meylan, *The Flute*, p. 112.
24. Jack Bymer, *Clarinet*. New York: Schirmer Books, 1976, pp. 10–11.
25. Quoted in Toff, *Development of the Modern Flute*, pp. 71–72.
26. Anthony Baines, *Woodwind Instruments and Their History*. New York: Dover Publications, 1991, p. 76.
27. Quoted in Gunther Joppig, *The Oboe and the Bassoon*. Portland,

OR: Amadeus Press, 1988, p. 18.

28. Quoted in Joppig, *The Oboe and the Bassoon,* p. 21.
29. Joppig, *The Oboe and the Bassoon,* p. 28.
30. Baines, *Woodwind Instruments and Their History,* p. 268.
31. Baines, *Woodwind Instruments and Their History,* pp. 277–79.
32. Philip Bate, *The Oboe.* New York: W.W. Norton, 1975, p. 60.
33. Bate, *The Oboe,* p. 92.
34. Baines, *Woodwind Instruments and Their History,* pp. 287, 289.
35. Bymer, *Clarinet,* p. 9.
36. Baines, *Woodwind Instruments and Their History,* p. 295.
37. Quoted in Bymer, *Clarinet,* p. 29.
38. Quoted in Baines, *Woodwind Instruments and Their History,* p. 331.
39. Quoted in Richard Ingham, *The Cambridge Companion to the Saxophone.* Cambridge, UK: Cambridge University Press, 1998, p. 16.
40. Quoted in Anthony Baines, *Brass Instruments: Their History and Development.* New York: Charles Scribner's Sons, 1978, pp. 254–55.
41. Galway, *Flute,* pp. 1–2.

Chapter Three: Brass
42. Trevor Herbert and John Wallace, eds., *The Cambridge Companion to Brass Instruments.* Cambridge, UK: Cambridge University Press, 1997, p. 1.
43. Quoted in Herbert and Wallace, eds., *The Cambridge Companion to Brass Instruments,* p. 19.
44. Edward Tarr, *The Trumpet.* London: B.T. Batsford, 1988, p. 19.
45. Tarr, *The Trumpet,* p. 20.
46. Quoted in Tarr, *The Trumpet,* p. 24.
47. Quoted in Herbert and Wallace, *The Cambridge Companion to Brass Instruments,* p. 43.
48. Tarr, *The Trumpet,* p. 47.
49. Quoted in Tarr, *The Trumpet,* p. 61.
50. Quoted in Herbert and Wallace, *The Cambridge Companion to Brass Instruments,* p. 50.
51. Quoted in Herbert and Wallace, *The Cambridge Companion to Brass Instruments,* pp. 56–57.

Chapter Four: Strings
52. Ashenafi Kebede, "A History Of Music," Music Cultures of the World. http://trigonal.ncat.edu.
53. Frederic V. Grunfeld, *The Art and Times of the Guitar.* London: Macmillan, 1969, p. 41.
54. Hortense Panum, *The Stringed Instruments of the Middle Ages.* New York: Da Capo Press, 1971, p. 91.
55. Robert Ruadh, "Gaelic Harps and Harpers in Ireland and Scotland." www.silcom.com.
56. Paul Huang, "The Harp," Instrumentally Speaking—Vienna Online, May 2000. www.geocities. com.
57. Grunfeld, *Art and Times of the Guitar,* p. 45.
58. Quoted in Grunfeld, *Art and Times of the Guitar,* p. 55.
59. Quoted in Panum, *Stringed Instruments of the Middle Ages,* p. 410.
60. Panum, *Stringed Instruments of the Middle Ages,* p. 423.

61. Grunfeld, *Art and Times of the Guitar,* p. 51.
62. Anna Alice Chapin, *The Heart of Music: The Story of the Violin.* Freeport, NY: Books for Libraries Press, 1971, p. 187.
63. Tony Bacon, *The Ultimate Guitar Book.* London: Dorling Kindersley, 1991, p. 8.
64. Quoted in Grunfeld, *Art and Times of the Guitar,* p. 109.
65. Quoted in Grunfeld, *Art and Times of the Guitar,* p. 235.

Chapter Five: Keyboards

66. C.F. Abdy Williams, *The Story of the Organ.* Detroit: Singing Tree Press, 1972, pp. 3–4.
67. Quoted in Peter Williams, *A New History of the Organ.* Bloomington: Indiana University Press, 1980, p. 20.
68. Bernard Sonnaillon and Stewart Spencer, trans., *King of Instruments.* New York: Rizzoli, 1984, p. 29.
69. Nicholas Thistlewaite and Geoffrey Webber, eds., *The Cambridge Companion to the Organ.* Cambridge, UK: Cambridge University Press, 1997, p. 8.
70. Quoted in Hans T. David and Arthur Mendel, eds., *The Bach Reader.* New York: W.W. Norton, 1966, p. 236.
71. David Crombie, *Piano.* San Francisco: GPI Books, 1995, p. 7.
72. Crombie, *Piano,* p. 11.
73. Crombie, *Piano,* p. 4.
74. Quoted in David Rowland, ed., *The Cambridge Companion to the Piano.* Cambridge, UK: Cambridge University Press, 1998, p. 17.
75. Quoted in Rowland, *Cambridge Companion to the Piano,* p. 22.
76. Rowland, *Cambridge Companion to the Piano,* p. 27.
77. Crombie, *Piano,* p. 33.

• For Further Reading •

Tony Bacon, *The Ultimate Guitar Book.* London: Dorling Kindersley, 1991. This story of the guitar includes profiles and information about rare, famous, and not-so-famous guitars with over 850 color pictures of Spanish, steel string, electric, and bass guitars.

Melvin Berger, *The Trumpet Book.* New York: Lothrop, Lee & Shepard, 1978. The story of the trumpet from its origins as a hollow reed to its use in modern music.

David Crombie, *Piano.* San Francisco: GPI Books, 1995. The history of pianos and piano players, illustrated with more than 150 stunning pictures of instruments throughout history.

The Diagram Group, *Musical Instruments of the World: An Illustrated Encyclopedia.* New York: Sterling Publishing, 1997. Hundreds of pictures and descriptions of rare and not-so-rare instruments.

Töm Klöwer, *The Joy of Drumming.* Diever, Holland: Binkey Kok Publications, 1997. A short history of drums and percussion instruments with over one hundred photos of drums, gongs, and other percussive instruments, along with explanations of how they are played and where they come from.

Bruce Koscielniak, *The Story of the Incredible Orchestra.* Boston: Houghton Mifflin, 2000. Describes the orchestra, the families of instruments that are played, and the individual instruments in each family.

Robert T. Levine, *Story of the Orchestra: Listen While You Learn About the Instruments, the Music, and the Composers Who Wrote the Music!* New York: Black Dog & Leventhal Publishers, 2000. A fascinating exploration of composers, musical definitions, and instruments of the orchestra, with a CD of short musical selections.

Josephine Parker, *Music from Strings.* Brookfield, CT: Millbrook Press, 1992. The richly illustrated story of lutes, violas, violins, guitars, harps, and even Indian sitars.

• Works Consulted •

Books

Anthony Baines, *Brass Instruments: Their History and Development.* New York: Charles Scribner's Sons, 1978. The trumpet, tuba, and other brass instruments through the Middle Ages, the Renaissance, and modern times.

———, *Woodwind Instruments and Their History.* New York: Dover Publications, 1991. A comprehensive look at the design, construction, and music of flutes, oboes, clarinets, and bassoons.

Philip Bate, *The Oboe.* New York: W.W. Norton, 1975. An exploration of the history, development, and construction of the oboe.

James Blades, *Percussion Instruments and their History.* London: Faber and Faber, 1974. One of the most comprehensive books ever written about drums and other idiophones, by the percussionist for the London Symphony Orchestra.

Jack Bymer, *Clarinet.* New York: Schirmer Books, 1976. The history, acoustic characteristics, and playing techniques of the clarinet.

Anna Alice Chapin, *The Heart of Music: The Story of the Violin.* Freeport, NY: Books for Libraries Press, 1971. A poetically written history of the violin, first published in 1906.

Hans T. David and Arthur Mendel, eds., *The Bach Reader.* New York: W. W. Norton, 1966. First published in 1945, this book details the life and times of Johann Sebastian Bach in his own words and those of his contemporaries by using source letters and documents gathered together in one volume for the first time.

James Galway, *Flute.* New York: Schirmer Books, 1982. The beautiful story of the flute written by a world-famous flautist who has recorded many classical, jazz, and pop music albums and has performed with the London Symphony Orchestra, the Berlin Philharmonic, and others.

Frederic V. Grunfeld, *The Art and Times of the Guitar.* London: Macmillan, 1969. An illustrated history of guitars and guitar players.

Mickey Hart with Jay Stevens, *Drumming at the Edge of Magic.* San Francisco: HarperCollins, 1990. The compelling story of percussion, drums, and drumming from the man who played drums for the Grateful Dead for more than thirty years.

Trevor Herbert and John Wallace, eds., *The Cambridge Companion to*

Brass Instruments. Cambridge, UK: Cambridge University Press, 1997. Covers a wide array of information concerning brass instruments in general, cornet, trumpet, and others.

Richard Ingham, *The Cambridge Companion to the Saxophone.* Cambridge, UK: Cambridge University Press, 1998. The history, technical development, and music of the saxophone from classical to jazz to rock.

Gunther Joppig, *The Oboe and the Bassoon.* Portland, OR: Amadeus Press, 1988. An interesting exploration of several woodwinds with photographs and drawings and discussion of tonal quality, variations, technique, and construction.

Colin Lawson, ed., *The Cambridge Companion to the Clarinet.* Cambridge, UK: Cambridge University Press, 1995. A thorough look at the clarinet, written for students and professionals with chapters on repertoire, history, guidance, and lessons.

Bernard S. Mason, *Drums, Tomtoms, and Rattles.* New York: Dover Publications, 1974. First published in 1938, this book discusses drums from around the world, the craft of drum making, dance drums, drumsticks, and idiophonic instruments.

Raymond Meylan, *The Flute.* Portland, OR: Amadeus Press, 1988. The story of the flute written by a well-known musicologist and performer with the Basel (Switzerland) Radio Symphony Orchestra.

Hortense Panum, *The Stringed Instruments of the Middle Ages.* New York: Da Capo Press, 1971. A comprehensive illustrated history of stringed instruments through the Greek, Roman, and medieval eras.

Layne Redmond, *When the Drummers Were Women.* New York: Three Rivers Press, 1997. An exploration of ancient cultures when women were the primary players of drums and used the instruments as a means of expressing spiritual unity and religious beliefs.

David Rowland, ed., *The Cambridge Companion to the Piano.* Cambridge, UK: Cambridge University Press, 1998. Essays on the development, players, and repertory of the piano.

Bernard Sonnaillon and Stewart Spencer, trans., *King of Instruments.* New York: Rizzoli, 1984. An extremely detailed and technical history of the organ with hundreds of photos and illustrations.

Keith Spence, *Living Music.* New York: Gloucester Press, 1979. The story of classical music, its forms, instruments, and history.

Edward Tarr, *The Trumpet.* London: B.T. Batsford, 1988. The history of the trumpet from pre-Roman times to the modern epoch.

Nicholas Thistlewaite and Geoffrey Webber, eds., *The Cambridge Companion to the Organ.* Cambridge, UK: Cambridge University Press, 1997. A compendium of several well-written essays concerning the mechanics, music, composers, and players of the "king of instruments."

Nancy Toff, *The Development of the Modern Flute*. New York: Taplinger Publishing, 1979. An exhaustive study of the development of the Boehm flute.

Charles L. White, *Drums Through the Ages*. Los Angeles: Sterling Press, 1960. Acquaints readers with ancient and modern percussion instruments and their uses.

C.F. Abdy Williams, *The Story of the Organ*. Detroit: Singing Tree Press, 1972. A colorful history of the organ written in Great Britain and first published in 1903.

Peter Williams, *A New History of the Organ*. Bloomington: Indiana University Press, 1980. A comprehensive study of the organ from Greek times to the present day, with eight chapters dedicated to the pre-Renaissance period alone.

Internet Sources

Pascal Baudar and Tony Rockliff, "Virtual Drums," 1994. www.cybertown.com. A website that allows the visitor to download a virtual drum set that can be played by tapping on the computer mouse.

Dan Beimborn, "A Brief History of the Mandolin," Mandolin Café, 2000. www.mandolincafe.com. A site about the mandolin by the Mandolin Café e-zine.

Henry Doktorski, "Birth of the Accordion," The Classical Free-Reed, Inc., 1998. http://trfn.clpgh.org. A website dedicated to the history of the accordion.

GuitarSite.com, 1999–2001. www.guitarsite.com. The biography of Andrés Segovia on an e-zine dedicated to guitars and guitar players with band bios, discussion forums, and countless links to musical styles and players.

Paul Huang, "The Cello," Instrumentally Speaking . . . The Cello—Vienna Online, August 2000. www.geocities.com. An article about the cello from a Vienna-based e-zine about music and culture.

——— "The Harp," Instrumentally Speaking . . . The Harp—Vienna Online," May 2000. www.geocities.com. An article about the modern harp from a Vienna-based e-zine about music and culture.

Ashenafi Kebede, "A History Of Music," Music Cultures of the World. http://trigonal.ncat.edu. A site with information about the history of several types of drums, percussion, and stringed instruments from Africa.

Marco Polo, "Kublai Khan in Battle, 1287," EyeWitness—History Through the Eyes of Those Who Lived It, 2000. www.ibiscom.com/khan.htm. The writings of the thirteenth-century Italian explorer on a website that features eyewitness accounts of historical events.

Bill Reese, "Thumbnail History of the Banjo." www.trussel.com. The history of the ancient African instrument now used primarily for bluegrass music.

Robert Ruadh, "Gaelic Harps and Harpers in Ireland and Scotland." www.silcom.com. A site with the history of the frame harp as it relates to the British Isles and Ireland.

Chris M. Slawecki, "Daniel Louis 'Satchmo' 'Pops' Armstrong," All About Jazz: Jazz Magazine and Resource, 1996–2001. www. allaboutjazz.com. An article about the life and musical accomplishments of Louis Armstrong.

• Index •

electric guitar, 76, 79–80
electric organ, 87
electric piano, 95
"Electric Spanish" guitar, 80
electronic keyboard, 95
embouchure, 30, 35
Ethiopia, 64

Fender, Leo, 80
fife, 31
Fifth Symphony, 59
first overtone, 49
flageolets, 31
flügelhorn, 58
Flute (Galway), 31, 32–33
Flute, The (Meylan), 28
flutes
    early forms of, 28–30
    how they are played, 30, 35
    improvements made to, 33–35
    music written for, 32
    popularity of, 33
foot pedals, 25
frame drums, 20
freeform jazz, 46
French horn, 59–60
"Frying Pan" guitar, 79

gagaku, 38
Galway, James, 31, 32
Gardiner, William, 42
Gibson A-4, 70
glissandi, 59
gongs, 17–18
Goodman, Benny, 42
gourd rattles, 15–16
grand piano, 94
Grateful Dead, 12, 25–26
Grunfeld, Frederic V., 64, 69
guasa, 17
guitars
    description of, 76
    early forms of, 76

electric, 76, 79–80
improvements made to, 78–79
instruction books for, 77
in jazz music, 79
materials used in, 76, 80
popularity of, 76, 77, 80
sounds made by, 76
versatility of, 76

Halévy, Jacques, 54
"Hallelujah Chorus" (Handel), 23
Hammond, Laurens, 87
Hammond organ, 87
Handel, George Frederic, 23, 54
"hand horn" technique, 59
harps
    categories of, 62
    concert grand, 67–68
    across cultures, 65–67
    early forms of, 65–67
    how they are played, 65
    materials used in, 67
    music written for, 68
    pedals for, 67–68
    shapes of, 65
    sounds made by, 68
harpsichords, 90–91
Hart, Mickey, 12–14, 26
hautbois, 39
Hawkins, John, 33
Haydn, Joseph, 33, 55, 59, 68, 71, 75
Heart of the Music, The (Chapin), 75
Hebenstreit, Pantaleon, 88–89
Hendrix, Jimi, 80
hichiriki, 38
"History of Music, A" (Kebede), 64
hunting calls, 56
hydraulos, 81

idiophones
    ancient beliefs about, 13
    across cultures, 12–14
    description of, 11

Morley, Thomas, 32
Morton, Jelly Roll, 96
mouthpiece, 28, 30, 35, 47–48
Mozart, Wolfgang Amadeus, 33, 42, 54, 55, 59, 68, 71, 75, 93–94

Naccara, 22
nay, 29
New History of the Organ, A (Peter Williams), 82
Nordelius, Hans, 26

oblique flute, 29–30
Oboe, The (Bate), 39
Oboe and the Bassoon, The (Joppig), 38
oboes
    across cultures, 38
    early forms of, 37–39
    how they are played, 35–37
    improvements made to, 39–40
    materials used in, 37
    for military purposes, 39
    popularity of, 39
    sounds made by, 39
octave, 33
Oliver, King, 57
orchestral horn, 59
Orfeo (Monteverde), 75
organs
    early forms of, 81–82
    how they are played, 83
    improvements made to, 83–84, 85, 87
    music written for, 85, 87
    origins of term, 82
    popularity of, 82
    sounds made by, 84–85
    used in churches, 82–83, 85
Orpheus, 63
orphica, 93
Osiris, 50
overtone series, 49

pallet box, 83
panpipe, 29
Parker, Charlie, 46
pedal harp, 67–68
pegbox, 72
percussion instruments,
    across cultures, 27
    description of, 11
    sounds made by, 27
    see also specific instruments
Percussion Instruments and Their History (Blades), 16
Piano (Crombie), 88–89
pianoforte, 92–93
pianos
    early forms of, 91–92
    improvements made to, 94
    invention of, 92
    in jazz music, 96
    music written for, 96
    popularity of, 94
    shapes and sizes of, 93
    sounds made by, 93
    Viennese-made, 93
piccolo trumpet, 54
pickup, 79
pipers, 38
player pianos, 94–96
plectrum, 90
Polo, Marco, 22
pommers, 38–39
portable piano, 93
Procol Harum, 87
psaltery, 62, 88

quinto, 23

ragtime, 96
rainmaker, 17
rattles, 15–16
Ravel, Maurice, 44
recorders, 32
Redmond, Layne, 20

• Picture Credits •

• About the Author •

Stuart A. Kallen is the author of more than 150 nonfiction books for children and young adults. He has written on topics ranging from the theory of
relativity to rock-and-roll history to life on the American frontier. In addition, Mr. Kallen has written award-winning children's videos and television
scripts. In his spare time he is a singer/songwriter/guitarist in San Diego,
California.